ENGLISH PREPOSITIONS

What? Where? How?

SC Gupta
BSc, MA, MCom, LLB, DLL, CAIIB

Kumkum Gupta
MA

Arihant Publications (India) LTD

Arihant Publications (India) Ltd.

卐 **ADMINISTRATIVE & PRODUCTION OFFICES**

Regd. Office

'Ramchhaya' 4577/15, Agarwal Road, Darya Ganj, New Delhi -110002
Tele: 011- 47630600, 43518550

Head Office

Kalindi, TP Nagar, Meerut (UP) - 250002
Tele: 0121-7156203, 7156204

卐 **SALES & SUPPORT OFFICES**

Agra, Ahmedabad, Bengaluru, Bareilly, Chennai, Delhi, Guwahati, Hyderabad, Jaipur, Jhansi, Kolkata, Lucknow, Nagpur & Pune

卐 **ISBN** : 978-81-8348-222-6

卐 **Price** : ₹ 65.00

Published by Arihant Publications (India) Ltd.

For further information about the books published by Arihant log on to www.arihantbooks.com or email to info@arihantbooks.com

Follow us on...

Preface

A preposition links nouns, pronouns and phrases to other words in a sentence. The word or phrase, introduces by the preposition, is called the object of the preposition. These are simple things; the definition and the rules usually everybody knows. Students are little concerned with the definitions, but the usage of the prepositions in various situations.

The book in your hand deals all about the prepositions. In almost all examinations, questions relating to preposition do appear. The book is aimed to make the students aware to the different kinds of prepositions used in different situations. We are sure that the book will surely help the students in making the correct use of the prepositions while writing and speaking english.

With all the good wishes....

Authors
129- South West Block
Near Eidgah
Alwar (Rajasthan) 301001

Contents

What is a Preposition?

A preposition is a word placed before a noun or a pronoun or a gerund. It denotes the relation, the person or thing referred by it has, with something else.

A preposition links **nouns, pronouns** and **phrases** to other words in a sentence. The word or phrase that the preposition introduces is called the **object** of the preposition. It should be noted that a personal pronoun following a preposition must be in the objcctivc casc.

There is one very simple rule about prepositions. And, unlike most rules, this rule has no exceptions:

A preposition is followed by a 'noun'. It is never followed by a verb.

By 'noun', we include :

(a) noun (dog, money, love);

(b) proper noun (name; *eg*, Pakistan, Rita);

(c) pronoun (him, you, her, they, us);

(d) noun group (my first love); and

(e) gerund (dancing, playing).

If we want a preposition followed by a verb, we must use the '-ing' form which is really **a gerund or verb in noun form.**

Read the following sentences :

(a) I would like to move now.

(b) He went to play.

Note: *In these sentences, 'to' is not a preposition. It is the part of the infinitive ('to move', 'to play').*

It should be understood well that verbs placed immediately after the preposition must be in gerund form :

(1) *He prevented me from drinking cold water.*

(2) *He insists on trying again.*

(3) *He was debarred from taking the examination.*

(4) *He succeeded in achieving his goal.*

(5) *They are afraid of losing the match.*

Look at the following sentences :

(1) The food is on the **table.**

(2) She lives in **China.**

(3) Mira is looking for **you.**

(4) The letter is under **your black book.**

(5) I ate before **coming.**

(6) He is swimming in the **river.**

In above sentences, all underlined words are **prepositions** and the words in bold type are **objects.**

A preposition serves to connect its object with the rest of the sentence. In doing so, a preposition indicates the relationship of the idea expressed in the prepositional phrase to the ideas expressed in the rest of the sentence.

Position of a Preposition

Prepositions normally precede nouns or pronouns. However, in certain cases, it is possible to move the preposition to the end of the sentence. For instance:

1. **When 'object' of the preposition is an interrogative pronoun; like—What, Who, Whom, Which, Where etc., the preposition takes the end or front position. For instance:**

   (i) What are you thinking of ?

   (ii) Who were you talking to ?

   (iii) What are you staring at ?

   (iv) Which of these chairs did you sit on?

   It used to be an ungrammatical thought to end a sentence with a preposition, but it is now accepted.

2. **When object of the preposition is relative pronoun, the preposition 'that' takes the end position. For instance:**

   (i) Here is the magazine that you asked for.

   (ii) This is the dish that she is fond of.

   (iii) This is the girl that I told you of.

   (iv) I know the colony that he lives in.

3. **When object of the preposition is infinitive (to + verb), the preposition is placed after the infinitive. For instance:**

   (i) This is a good hotel **to stay** at.

   (ii) I need a pencil **to write** with.

   (iii) It is a beautiful house **to live** in.

   (iv) This is a ball **to play** with.

4. **In some sentences, the relative pronoun is hidden. For instance:**

   (i) This is the house(where) I lived in.

   (ii) This is the girl (that) I told you of.

5. **In some miscellaneous sentences, the preposition is attached with the verb :**

   (i) I hate being laughed at.

   (ii) This is the matter I insist on.

   (iii) He likes being looked at.

   (iv) He is known all the world over.

6. **In some cases, the preposition comes in the beginning. These are usually interrogative sentences:**

   (i) By which train did you come?

   (ii) For whom were the instructions given?

   (iii) In which class do you read?

   (iv) To whom were you talking?

Kinds of Prepositions

Prepositions can be classified in the following categories :

1. **Simple Prepositions :** At, in, for, from, of, off, on, out, till, to, up, with, through, down, by, etc., are some of the prepositions that are included in this category. These are most commonly used prepositions.

2. **Compound Prepositions :** These are usually formed by prefixing 'a' or 'be' to a noun, an adjective or an adverb:

about	beside	inside
along	below	outside
amidst	beneath	within
among	between	without
aloud	beyond	underneath

3. **Phrasal Prepositions :** These are formed by joining two or more words:

along with	in addition to	in place of
because of	in case of	in spite of
by means of	in course of	owing to
for the sake of	with reference to	in comparison to
in favour of	with regard to	instead of
in accordance with	with respect to	according to
in lieu of	in front of	in consequence of

4. **Participial Prepositions :** When present participles are used without any noun or pronoun attached to them, they are called participial prepositions. Most commonly used present participles are:

   Concerning, Pending, Regarding, Considering, Touching, During, Notwithstanding, etc., see below:

   (a) **Pending** enquiry into the matter, he was transferred from the office.

   (b) **Considering** the quality, the prices are reasonable.

   (c) **Notwithstanding** the protest made by the people, he was arrested by the police.

(d) **Regarding** your suggestions, we are to inform you that we cannot allow any relaxation further.

Prepositional Phrase : A phrase beginning with a preposition can be referred to as a prepositional phrase. The prepositional phrases are underlined in the following examples:

(a) He owns the hotel on the corner.

(b) We are waiting for her.

(c) She has read many books about flying.

In the first example, the noun **'corner'** is the object of the preposition **'on'.** In the second example, the personal pronoun **'her'** is the object of the preposition **'for'.** It can be seen that the personal pronoun **'her'** is in the objective case. In the third example, the gerund **'flying'** is the object of the preposition **'about'.**

Some Important Prepositions

At/In/On

These are very commonly used prepositions :

Note the use of these prepositions in reference of 'Time' :

(i) **'At'** is used to introduce a PRECISE TIME;

(ii) **In** is used for MONTHS, YEARS, CENTURIES and LONG PERIODS; and

(iii) **On** is used for DAYS and DATES:

AT (Precise Time)	**IN (Months, Years, Centuries and Long Periods)**	**ON (Days, Dates)**
at 3 o'clock	in May	on Sunday
at 10 : 30 am	in summer	on Tuesdays
at noon	in the summer	on 6th March
at dinner time	in 1990	on 25th Jan. '07
at bedtime	in the 1990s	on Christmas Day

at sunrise	in the next century	on Independence Day
at sunset	in the Ice Age	on my birthday
at the moment	in the past/future	on New Year's Eve

Look at the following examples :

(1) I have a meeting at 10 am.

(2) That shop closes at midnight.

(3) Richa went home at lunchtime.

(4) Where will you be on Independence Day?

(5) Do you think we will go to Saturn in the future?

(6) There should be a lot of progress in the next century.

(7) Do you work on Sunday?

(8) Her birthday is on 26th April.

Note the use of prepositions of time, 'at/in' in the following expressions:

Expression	**Example**
at night	The stars shine at night.
at the weekend	I don't usually work at the weekend.
at Christmas/Easter	I stay with my family at Christmas.
at the same time	We finished the test at the same time.
at present	He's not in home at present.

Note the use of prepositions of time—'in and on' in these common expressions:

in	**on**
in the morning	on Tuesday morning
in the mornings	on Saturday mornings
in the afternoon(s)	on Sunday afternoon
in the evening(s)	on Monday evening

Important : We should not use; 'at, in, on' with 'last, next, every':

(i) I went to Mexico last May. (not 'in' last May)

(ii) He's coming back next Sunday. (not 'on' next Sunday)

(iii) I go home every Easter. (not 'at' every Easter)

(iv) We'll call you this evening. (not 'in' this evening)

Note the use of these prepositions in reference of 'Place':

(i) **'At'** is used to denote a POINT,

(ii) **'In'** is used for an ENCLOSED SPACE, and

(iii) **'On'** is used for a SURFACE.

AT (POINT)	**IN (ENCLOSED SPACE)**	**ON (SURFACE)**
at the corner	in the garden	on the wall
at the bus stop	in Delhi	on the ceiling
at the door	in India	on the door
at the top of the page	in a box	on the cover
at the end of the road	in my pocket	on the floor
at the entrance	in my wallet	on the carpet
at the crossroads	in a building	on the menu
at the address	in a car	on a page

Look at the following examples :

(1) Rima is waiting for you at the bus stop.

(2) The shop is at the end of the lane.

(3) I live on the 4th floor at 21, Diamond Street in Kolkata.

(4) When will you arrive at the school?

(5) Do you work in a company?

(6) I have a meeting in Delhi .

(7) Do you live in India ?

(8) Saturn is in the Solar System.

(9) The author's name is on the cover of the book.

(10) There are no prices on this menu.

(11) You are standing on my foot.

(12) There was a "No Smoking" sign on the wall.

Please note that these three prepositions are most commonly used in writing and speaking, so the students must learn the use of these prepositions well.

At/ In/ To/ Into

1. **'At'** shows stationary position or existing state while **'In'** shows movement:
   (i) She is at home.
   (ii) The train is in motion.
2. **'At'** is used for small place, town etc. while **'In'** is used for big place, town, city, country, etc.:
   (i) He lives at Alwar in Rajasthan.
   (ii) A temple is situated at Madurai in Chennai.
3. **'At'** is used for denoting point of time and **'In'** is used for denoting period of time:
   (i) The train will arrive at six in the morning.
   (ii) He will meet you in the morning.
4. **'In'** shows existing state of things while **'Into'** shows movement:
   (i) He jumped into the river.
   (ii) There are three students in the class.
   (iii) They climbed into the lorry.
   (iv) He is swimming in the river.

   In can also be used as an adverb :

   'Come in' means 'to enter'; Get in (into the train).
5. **To/Into : These are used in the following manner:**

   To :
   (i) In the direction of : Turn to the right.
   (ii) Destination : I am going to Jaipur.
   (iii) Until : from Monday to Friday; five minutes to ten.
   (iv) Compared with : They prefer hockey to soccer.
   (v) With indirect object : Please give it to me.
   (vi) As part of infinitive : I like to ski; he wants to help.
   (vii) In order to : We went to the store to buy soap.

Into :

(i) To the inside of : We stepped into the room.

(ii) Change of condition : The boy changed into a man.

On/Onto

'On' can be used for both existing position and movement. For example:

(i) He was sitting on his bag.

(ii) Snow fell on the hills.

(iii) His number is on the gate.

(iv) He went on board.

'On' can also be used as an adverb:

(a) Go on. Come on.

'Onto' is used when there is movement involving a change of level :

(i) People climbed onto their roofs.

(ii) He lifted her onto the table.

With/By

'With' is used for instruments and **'By'** is used for agents:

(i) The snake was killed by him with a stick.

(ii) The letter was written by Suresh with a pencil.

Since/For/From

'Since' is often used with present perfect or past perfect tense. **'Since'** is used for point of time and never for place; for example—Since 6 O'clock/last night/last Monday; since morning/evening/Monday/ January/2005, etc.:

(i) It has been raining since two O'clock.

(ii) He had been ill since Monday.

Note : ***'Since'*** *can also be used as an adverb:*

(i) He left school in 1983. I haven't seen him since.

(ii) It is two years since I last saw Tom.

'For' is used for a period of time; for instance—for two hours/two days/two years/a long time/some time/for ever etc.:

(i) Boil it for two hours.

(ii) He lived in this house for six months.

'For' is also used with a present perfect tense or past perfect tense, for an action which extends up to the time of speaking:

(i) He has worked here for a year.

(ii) It has been raining for two hours.

(iii) He worked for three hours.

'From' is normally used with 'to' or 'till/until' :

(i) Most people work from eight to six.

'From' can also be used for place :

(i) He is from Mumbai.

(ii) Where do you come from ?

For/During

During is used to introduce known period of time, *i.e.,* periods known by name; such as—Christmas, Easter or periods which have been already defined:

1. during the middle ages,
2. during the summer,
3. during his childhood:

(i) It rained all Sunday but stopped raining during the night.

(ii) She was ill for a week, and during that week, she ate nothing.

'For' may be used to denote purpose and may also be used before known periods. For instance:

(i) I went there for the summer.

(ii) I rented my house for the holidays.

(iii) I rented my car for summer only.

'For' has various other uses :

(i) He asked for ten.I paid six for it.

(ii) I bought one for Kuku.

(iii) He has been ill for three days.

Below/Under/Beneath

'Below' and **'under'**, both mean lower than (in level) and sometimes either can be used. But **'under'** usually denotes physical contact and **'below'** denotes space between the things :

(i) He put the books under the pillow.

(ii) He placed the lamp below the almirah.

(iii) They live below us. (This means, we live at the second floor while they live at the first floor).

(iv) I was wearing a sweater also under the jacket.

'Below' and **'under'** may also mean junior in rank.

(v) He is under me. (This means, I am superior to him)

(vi) He is working under me.

'Below' is used for meaning opposite to above.

(i) The temperature can fall below 15 degree Celsius.

(ii) Rainfall has been below average this year.

'Beneath' is used to denote something which is under another thing :

(i) I could see the muscles of his shoulders beneath his T-shirt.

(ii) I found pleasure in sitting beneath the trees.

(iii) ...the frozen grass crunching beneath his feet.

'Beneath' could also mean 'unworthy as per status' or 'in lower strata in social class'. For instance :

It is beneath his dignity to beg for money. (This means, it is unworthy of him.)

She married beneath her. (This means, she married into a lower social class.)

In/Within

'In' means the maximum time limit, while **'within'** means the period upto which the work will be completed. **'Within** a particular length of time' means before the expiry of that length of time, while **'in'** refers the maximum time required for the completion of the job :

(i) I will complete the work in a month.

(ii) I can repair the car within two hours.

(iii) He will write a book in three months.

(iv) He can solve this question within an hour.

Ago/Before

'Ago' is used for past events while **'before'** is used in reference to two events:

(i) He came three days ago.

(ii) The train had left before he reached the station .

Beside/Besides

'Beside' and **'Besides'** have altogether different meanings. Don't confuse **'beside'** with **'besides'**.

'Beside' means 'at the side of' :

(i) He was sitting beside Sarla.

(ii) We camped beside a lake.

'Besides' means 'in addition to' or 'as well as' :

(i) He has a car besides a motor cycle.

(ii) Besides doing the cooking, I help Ram.

Between/Among

'Between' is normally used for two things or persons, but it can also be used when we have a definite number in mind and there is a close relationship or association within them:

(i) He distributed his property between his two sons.

(ii) Luxembourg lies between Belgium, Germany and France.

(iii) A treaty was signed between the three parties.

(iv) He inserted a needle between the close petals of a flower.

'Among' is usually used for more than two persons or things, when we have no definite number in mind:

(i) He was happy to be among friends again.

(ii) He distributed his property among the poor.

Among/Amongst

Both have the same meaning. Either of them can be used if followed by 'the'. If followed by a word beginning with a vowel, **'amongst'** be used. The use of **'amongst'** is usually found in literary writings:

(i) He distributed the toffees among/amongst the poor.

(ii) He distributed the toffees amongst us.

Of/Off

'Of' is used in the following situations referring :

(i) Location : east of here; the middle of the road.

(ii) Possession : a friend of mine; the sound of music.

(iii) Part of a group : one of us; a member of the team.

(iv) Measurement: a cup of milk; two meters of snow.

'Off' is used in the following manner:

(i) Not on; away from : Please keep off the grass.

(ii) At some distance from : There are islands off the coast.

(iii) He is off duty now.

(iv) He jumped off the tower.

(v) He is a member of our family.

(vi) She is a member of our society.

(vii) She parked her car in the middle of the road.

Above/Over

'Above' and **'over'** both mean 'higher than' and sometimes either can be used:

(i) The helicopter hovered above/over us.

(ii) White flags were waved above/over the buildings.

But **'over'** also means 'covering'/'on the other side of'/ 'across':

(i) I put a cloth over her.

(ii) He lives over this mountain.

(iii) There is a bridge over the railway line.

(iv) He put a blanket over the dead body.

'Above' can have none of these meanings.

'Over' can mean higher in rank:

He is over me.(It means that he is my immediate boss.)

'Over' is also used with meals/food/drink :

(i) We had a chat over a cup of tea. (while drinking tea)

(ii) The matter was decided over the lunch.

'Above' is also used for meaning 'earlier'or 'previous' :

(i) He lives at the above address. (This means that the address is previously mentioned.)

(ii) For details, please see (page-1) above. (This means that the details are previously mentioned.)

Make of/Make from

Both refer to the material used.

'Make of' is used when the shape of the material is not changed:

(i) A note book is made of papers.

(ii) A house is made of bricks.

'Make from' is used when shape of the material has undergone a total change:

(i) Butter is made **from** milk.

(ii) Paper is made **from** grass.

In/With

'In' is used in the following situations:

(i) **Place, thought of as an area: in** London; **in** Europe.

(ii) **Within a location: in** the room; **in** the building.

(iii) **Large units of time:** That happened **in** March, **in** 1992.

(iv) **Within a certain time:** I will return **in** an hour.

(v) **By means of:** Write in pencil; Speak **in** English.

(vi) **When there is a condition : in** doubt; **in** a hurry; **in** secret.

(vii) **A member of :** He is **in** the orchestra; **in** the navy.

(viii) **When one has to describe what someone is wearing:** The boy **in** the blue shirt.

(ix) **With reference to:** lacking **in** ideas; rich **in** oil.

'With' is used in the following situations:

(i) **Accompanying:** He came with her; I have my keys **with** me.

(ii) **Having; containing :** Here is a book with a map of the island.

(iii) **By means of; using :** I repaired the shoes with glue.

(iv) **When describing manner : with** pleasure; **with** ease; **with** difficulty.

(v) **Because of :** We were paralyzed with fear.

(vi) **When describing an agreement :** I agree with you.

Opposite/In front of

'Opposite' is used for meaning antonym and 'position in front'. **'In front of'** always means front position. See the following examples :

Supposing, *Ram and Shyam are having meal. Ram is sitting at one side of the table and Shyam at the other side.* We will say :

(i) Ram is sitting opposite to Shyam.(Ram is facing Shyam.)

(ii) People living on one side of a street will talk of the houses on the other side as the houses opposite rather than the houses in front of us.

(iii) His house is opposite to ours

'In front of' is used in the following ways :

(i) He parked the car in front of the hotel.

(ii) He put the plates on the table in front of us.

By and Before

'**By** a time/**by** a date' usually implies before that time or date:

The train starts at 7 : 15 am so you had better be at the station by 7 : 00 am.

'By + a time expression' structure is often used with future perfect tense:

By the end of July, I'll have read all those books.

'Before' can be used as a preposition, conjunction or as an adverb.

(i) Before signing this agreement, let us discuss each and every point thread bare. (preposition)

(ii) Before you sign this, you can discuss it with your father. (conjunction)

(iii) I've seen her somewhere before. (adverb)

After/Afterwards

'After/Afterwards' must be followed by a noun, pronoun or gerund :

(i) After breakfast, he ordered a taxi.

(ii) Don't run immediately after a meal/after eating.

(iii) Don't have a meal and run immediately after it.

If we do not like to use a noun/pronoun or gerund, we cannot use **'after'** but we can use **'afterwards'** or **'then'**:

(i) Don't have a meal and run immediately afterwards.

(ii) They bathed and afterwards played games.

'Afterwards' can be used at either end of the clause and can be modified by; **soon, immediately, not long,** etc.:

(i) Soon afterwards, I got a call.

(ii) I got a call not long afterwards.

But/Except

Both have the same meaning and are usually interchangeable.

After nobody/none/nothing/nowhere, etc., usually **'but'** is used:

(i) Nobody but Shyam knew the way.

(ii) Nothing but the best is sold in our shop.

'Except' is used when the prepositional phrase comes later in a sentence.

Look at the following example.

Nobody knew the way except Shyam.

Note: *After 'but' and 'except', bare infinitive (infinitive without 'to') is used.*

To/Towards

The preposition **'to'** indicates movement with the aim of a specific destination, which can be a place or an event. For example:

(i) I'm going to USA tomorrow.

(ii) I need to go to the bank.

(iii) Can you tell me the way to the station?

(iv) Are you going to the party?

(v) I've never been to a cricket match.

(vi) What time did you go to work?

Note: *'Upto' is often used to express movement of a person. For example:*

She came upto me and asked what the time was.

The preposition **'to'** is sometimes used to indicate a specific position, especially if a person or object is facing something, *e.g.* :

(i) There's a door to your left.

(ii) He stood with his back to the window.

The preposition **'towards'** indicates movement in a particular direction:

(i) She was carrying a suitcase and walking towards the railway station.

(ii) He hit the ball towards the goal.

(iii) She pointed towards the door.

(iv) Everyone sitting in the room turned towards me.

Note: *See the contrast in the following two examples:*

(i) I'm going to New York for a meeting.

(ii) I think we're heading towards New York now, we must have gone wrong.

In the first example, **'to'** refers a specific destination. In the second example, with **'towards'**, the direction of movement is more specifically indicated.

Note: *Occasionally, **'towards'** is also used to indicate position, but this is a position in relation to a particular direction from the point of view of the speaker. For example:*

(i) She was sitting towards the back of the room.

(ii) Tom stood with his back towards the door.

Through/Into

The preposition **'through'** refers to movement within a space which can be thought of as three-dimensional, for example:

(i) We couldn't get the new sofa through the door.

(ii) They drove through some spectacular countryside.

(iii) The canal flows through the city centre.

(iv) You won't be able to see it unless you look through the binoculars.

'Through' usually suggests movement across an entire space, from one side of something to another, for example:

He cut through the wire.

The preposition **into** refers to movement from outside to the inside of a three dimensional space, *e.g.:*

(i) We got into the back of the car.

(ii) She reached into her bag and found the keys.

With certain verbs, into can be used to express the idea of movement in the direction of something, often resulting in actually hitting it, as in the example given below.

(i) He looked straight into her eyes.

(ii) She swerved and crashed into the fence.

Across/Over/Along

The prepositions; **'across'** and **'over'** are used to talk about movement from one side of a place to another. They usually refer to movement in relation to places which can be thought of as two-dimensional, such as surfaces (*e.g.*, a lawn) or lines (*e.g.*, a river), for example:

(i) I'll jump over the wall and open the gate.

(ii) The aircraft flew low over the lake.

(iii) How are we going to get across the stream?

(iv) It's the first time I've flown across the Atlantic.

'Over' also functions as a preposition, expressing position. It often has a meaning similar to the preposition 'above', for example :

(i) There was a mirror above/over the sink.

One of its core uses, however, is to express position in relation to a two-dimensional surface, for example :

(ii) A white tablecloth was spread over the table.

Or to show when something is positioned on the opposite side of a line, *e.g.*, road, bridge, etc.:

(iii) The hotel is **over** the bridge.

'Across' is sometimes used to express position in relation to something which stretches from one side of a place to another, for example :

(i) There was a barrier across the road.

And like **'over'**, it is also used when something is positioned on the opposite side of a place in relation to the speaker. For example :

The bank is across the street.

The preposition **'along'** is used to show movement following a line. For example :

(i) We walked along the river.

(ii) I followed Mr Jackson along the corridor.

(iii) Well-wishers began placing flowers along the railings.

It is also sometimes used to show a specific position in relation to a line. For example:

Somewhere along the path, there's a signpost.

Or to show when a group of things is positioned in a line next to something. For example :

There were plenty of restaurants along the river front.

Prepositions with Nouns, Adjectives, and Verbs

Prepositions are sometimes so firmly attached to certain other words that they have practically become one word.

Nouns

Nouns followed by prepositions : The following are some examples of nouns which are usually followed by certain prepositions. In the case of phrases which are idioms, the meanings of the phrases are indicated in brackets:

Against

take precautions against

For

have affection for
have compassion for
a reason for
have respect for
have a talent for
pave the way for (prepare for)
make allowances for
an excuse for
have a reputation for
have sympathy for
lie in wait for (ambush)

From

absence from

In

have confidence in
have an interest in
make progress in
have faith in
take part in

Into

have insight into

Of

have an abhorrence of
take advantage of
take command of
an acknowledgment of
take care of
evidence of

an example of

an excess of

make a fool of

make fun of (ridicule)

have an impression of

a lack of

neglect of

a number of

a pair of

be part of

a possibility of

make a practice of (do often)

a proof of

a quantity of

recognition of

a recollection of

a result of

run the risk of (risk)

catch sight of (see suddenly)

a sign of

a survey of

a symbol of

a symptom of

a token of

make use of

a way of

wash one's hands of (stop caring about something and dealing with it.)

On

an attack on

dependence on

make an impression on

play a joke on

shed light on (to explain)

have pity on

To

have access to

pay attention to

an objection to

a reply to

a response to

lay siege to (besiege)

shut one's eyes to (to deliberately ignore a problem)

Toward or Towards

animosity toward(s)

an attitude toward(s)

With

have a connection with

find fault with (criticize)

fall in love with

change places with

Adjectives and Verbs

Adjectives and verbs in the passive voice followed by prepositions :

In some cases, different prepositions can be used at the same place without causing a change in meaning of the sentence. For instance, both the following examples have the same meaning:

(1) I was angry at them.

(2) I was angry with them.

However, in many cases, use of different prepositions causes a change in meaning. For instance, the past participle **'protected'** is typically followed by the preposition **'from'.** However, like many other past participles, **'protected'** may be followed by the preposition **'by'** also, where **'by'** serves to introduce the performer of the action expressed by the past participle:

(1) The city is protected from the soldiers.

(2) The city is protected by the soldiers.

The first example indicates that the soldiers are a threat to the city; whereas, the second example indicates that the soldiers are protecting the city.

The following are the examples of predicate adjectives and past participles of verbs in the passive voice which are usually followed by certain prepositions. In addition, it should be kept in mind that most verbs in the passive voice can be followed by a phrase beginning with the preposition **'by'**:

About

anxious about   concerned about   curious about   depressed about

doubtful about   enthusiastic about   excited about   happy about

pleased about   wrong about   worried about

At

adept at   alarmed at   amazed at   overjoyed at

surprised at   shocked at

Between

torn between

By

accompanied by caused by guided by manufactured by obsessed by written by

For

blamed for eligible for famous for fit for known for late for noted for praised for punished for qualified for ready for responsible for ripe for sorry for suitable for

From

absent from apart from derived from descended from detached from different from distinct from exempt from far from isolated from omitted from protected from removed from safe from separated from

In

absorbed in disappointed in engaged in immersed in interested in involved in

Of

accused of afraid of ashamed of aware of capable of certain of composed of conscious of convinced of deprived of devoid of fond of ignorant of independent of jealous of proud of regardless of reminded of sure of suspicious of suspected of terrified of tired of worthy of

On

based on dependent on intent on

To

acceptable to accessible to accustomed to adapted to addicted to adjacent to attached to attributable to close to committed to comparable to dedicated to detrimental to devoted to due to equal to equivalent to essential to exposed to faithful to favourable to foreign to impervious to indifferent to

indispensable to	inferior to	kind to	loyal to
obedient to	obliged to	oblivious to	opposed to
parallel to	partial to	peculiar to	preferable to
prior to	proportional to	reconciled to	reduced to
related to	relative to	relevant to	resigned to
resistant to	restricted to	senior to	sensitive to
similar to	subject to	subordinate to	suited to
superior to	susceptible to	tied to	next to

Toward or Towards

protective toward(s)

With

acquainted with	affiliated with	associated with	besieged with
compared with	compatible with	confronted with	consistent with
covered with	cursed with	exasperated with	familiar with
finished with	identified with	infatuated with	patient with
pleased with	satisfied with	synonymous with	threatened with

Prepositions Used in Idioms

Below are examples of some idioms consisting of prepositional phrases. The meaning of each idiom is indicated after the colon:

At

not **at** all	:	not in any way
at all times	:	always
at any rate	:	whatever happens
keep someone **at** arm's length	:	avoid becoming closely involved with someone
at close quarters	:	very near
at one's disposal	:	to be used as one wishes
at a distance	:	not near
at fault	:	causing something wrong
at first	:	at the beginning
see **at** a glance	:	see immediately
at hand	:	near; readily available
at last	:	finally, after some delay
at a loss	:	uncertain about what to do or say; be puzzled
at the mercy of	:	without defence against
at the moment	:	now
at once	:	immediately
at present	:	now
at rest	:	not moving
at risk	:	threatened by danger or loss
at short notice	:	with little warning
at stake	:	to be won or lost
at a stretch	:	continuously
at that rate	:	under those circumstances
at this point	:	at this place; at this moment
at the wheel	:	in control

Behind

behind the scene : (of persons) influencing events secretly; (in a theatre) behind the stage

behind schedule : not on time

Beside

be **beside** oneself : lose one's self-control

beside the point : irrelevant

Between

read **between** the lines : deduce a meaning that is not actually expressed

Beyond

beyond help : unable to be helped

beyond a joke : too annoying to be amusing; passing the limits of what is reasonable as a joke

beyond reproach : perfect; blameless

By

by accident : not deliberately

by all means : by any possible method

bit **by** bit : gradually

by chance : by accident; without planning; result of a chance

by courtesy of : with the help or permission of

win **by** default : win because of lack of competition

by degrees : gradually

perform **by** ear : perform (music) by listening to the sound, without referring to written music

by hand : without the use of machinery

by heart : from memory

little **by** little : gradually

by means of : by using

by mistake : accidentally

by no means : not at all

one **by** one	:	one at a time
by oneself	:	alone; without help
side **by** side	:	beside one another
by the way	:	incidentally (it is used to introduce an unrelated topic of conversation)
by word of mouth	:	orally

For

once and **for** all	:	for the last time (*e.g.,* it is used when giving someone a final warning)
for certain	:	definitely; without doubt
for a change	:	for the sake of variety
for example	:	as an illustration
for fun	:	for the sake of enjoyment
for good	:	permanently
for good measure	:	in addition to the necessary amount
for instance	:	for example; as an illustration
for keeps	:	(colloquial) permanently
for a living	:	as a profession
for now	:	temporarily
run **for** office	:	compete for an elected position
for one thing	:	because of one reason (out of several reasons)
for the sake of	:	for the benefit of; for the purpose of
for sale	:	intended to be sold
for sure	:	definitely (more colloquial than 'for certain')
food **for** thought	:	something which makes one think
play **for** time	:	delay doing something in the hope that the situation will improve
for the time being	:	until some other arrangement is made
ask **for** trouble	:	act in a dangerous or foolish way
for a while	:	for a period of time
word **for** word	:	exactly as said or written

From

from afar	:	from a distance
from all sides	:	from all directions
from head to foot	:	(of a person) completely; all over
from scratch	:	from the beginning
from time to time	:	occasionally

In

in addition to	:	as well as
in advance	:	before
be **in** agreement with	:	have the same opinion as
in any case	:	whatever happens
in brief	:	in a few words
in bulk	:	(of goods) in large amounts and not in packages
be **in** charge of	:	have responsibility for
in common	:	shared by all members of a group
in control	:	having the power to direct something
in the course of	:	during
in danger	:	likely to be harmed
in a daze	:	unable to think clearly; confused
in debt	:	owing money
in demand	:	(of goods or persons) desired by many people
in depth	:	(investigate something) thoroughly
in detail	:	(explain something) thoroughly
in disgrace	:	(something/someone) regarded with disapproval because of having done something wrong
in the distance	:	far away
in doubt	:	uncertain
in duplicate	:	so that there are two identical copies (of a document)
in earnest	:	seriously; in a determined way

in effect	: (of rules) operating
in the end	: finally
in fact	: in reality; really
in fashion	: fashionable; accepted as being the most desirable and up to date
in favour of	: supporting (an idea)
in flames	: burning with visible flames
in a flash	: very quickly; suddenly
in full	: without omitting anything
in general	: usually; as a whole
hand **in** hand	: (of persons) holding hands; (of related situations) occurring together
in a hurry	: trying to accomplish something quickly
in jest	: as a joke
in kind	: (payment) in goods rather than in money
in itself	: without reference to anything else; in its own nature
in league with	: (of persons) joined together with (usually for a dishonest purpose)
be **in** the limelight	: be the focus of attention; receive great publicity
in the long-run	: in the end; eventually
in the long-term	: looking ahead to the distant future
leave someone **in** the lurch	: abandon someone in a difficult situation
be **in** the minority	: be in the smaller of two groups
in mint condition	: (of manufactured goods) perfect; brand-new
in a minute	: soon
in a moment	: soon; quickly
set something **in** motion	: start something going
nip something **in** the bud	: put an end to something before it gets properly started
in no time	: very soon; very quickly

in order of	:	arranged according to
in order to	:	for the purpose of
in part	:	to some degree
in particular	:	especially
in power	:	(of a political party) holding office
in practice	:	able to do something well because of recent practice; in reality (opposite of 'in theory')
in print	:	(of a book) printed and available from the publisher
in private	:	not in front of other people; in camera
in public	:	openly; not in private
in reality	:	really
in reserve	:	saved for later use
in retrospect	:	looking back over past events
in return for	:	as repayment for
be **in** the right	:	be correct
in season	:	(of fruit or vegetables) readily available at that time of year
in a second	:	soon; quickly
in short supply	:	scarce; not easily obtainable
in sight	:	able to be seen
in stock	:	(of goods at a store) present and available
in that case	:	if that is true
in theory	:	ideally; according to theoretical considerations
be **in** time	:	not be late
in touch with	:	communication with; informed about
in triplicate	:	so that there are three identical copies (of a document)
be **in** trouble	:	be in a difficult situation; be blamed or punished for doing something wrong; be in hot waters

in tune	:	at the correct pitch
act **in** unison	:	act together
in vain	:	without success
in the vicinity of	:	near
once **in** a while	:	occasionally
in words of one syllable	:	(explain something) clearly and simply
in working order	:	able to function properly
in the wrong	:	responsible for an error; guilty

Inside

inside out	:	with the inner side out; thoroughly; out and in

Into

paint oneself **into** a corner	:	take a course of action which greatly narrows one's future choices of action
go **into** hiding	:	hide oneself
get **into** a rut	:	get into a fixed and uninteresting way of life
get **into** trouble	:	get into a difficult situation; do something deserving blame or punishment

Of

of course	:	certainly; as one would expect; as everyone knows
hard **of** hearing	:	somewhat deaf; partialley hearing impared
next **of** kin	:	nearest relative or relatives
of one's own accord	:	voluntarily; on one's own initiative
of one's own free will	:	voluntarily; by choice
one's point **of** view	:	one's opinion about something
right **of** way	:	public right to use a path or road; (of road traffic) right to proceed before others
rule **of** thumb	:	a simple way to calculate what procedure to follow, based on extensive experience, rather than on theoretical considerations

Off

go **off** the air	:	(of radio or television) stop broadcasting
off duty	:	not engaged in one's regular work
off one's hands	:	no longer one's responsibility
off and on	:	from time to time; occasionally
off the record	:	say something privately, that is not to be officially recorded
off the track	:	following a wrong line of thought or action

On

on account of	:	because of
be **on** the air	:	(of radio or television) be in the process of broadcasting
on the alert	:	ready to act
be **on** all fours	:	(of a person) be on hands and knees
on the average	:	usually; normally
on behalf of	:	for; in the interests of
on board	:	on a ship or airplane
on business	:	as part of one's work
on condition that	:	only if; provided that
on demand	:	when asked for
on display	:	being exhibited
on duty	:	engaged in one's regular work
on fire	:	burning
to go **on** foot	:	to walk
be **on** one's guard	:	be alert and ready to meet an attack
on hand	:	available
on loan	:	lent and not yet returned
shoot **on** location	:	(of a movie/tele-serial) film in natural surroundings, not in a studio
on the lookout	:	watchful
put something **on** the map	:	cause something to become well-known

get **on** one's nerves	:	annoy; irritate
on no account	:	absolutely not
on the one hand	:	(used to introduce one side of an argument)
on one's own	:	alone; without help
act **on** one's own initiative	:	act independently, without orders from anyone else
on order	:	requested but not yet delivered
on the other hand	:	(used to introduce a contrasting side of an argument)
act **on** principle	:	do something to support a policy
on purpose	:	deliberately
go **on** record	:	say something which is to be officially recorded
on sale	:	being sold at a price lower than usual
on schedule	:	at the correct time; as planned or predicted
on second thoughts	:	after thinking further about something
on a shoestring budget	:	with a very small amount of money
be **on** the spot	:	be where important events are taking place; be placed in an awkward situation
on the spur of the moment	:	on a sudden impulse
go off **on** a tangent	:	change suddenly to a new line of thought or action
on time	:	at the correct time
walk **on** tiptoe	:	walk on the toes and balls of the feet
accept something **on** trust	:	accept something without proof
on the verge of	:	very close to; about to
on the whole	:	taking everything into consideration

Out of

out of the blue	:	unexpectedly
out of breath	:	(after running) panting from shortage of oxygen
out of character	:	unlike a person's known character
out of control	:	not able to be regulated or guided
out of danger	:	safe
out of date	:	no longer used; old-fashioned; (of news) no longer true
out of debt	:	having paid one's debts
be **out of** one's depth	:	be unable to handle a situation because of lack of experience
out of doors	:	in the open air; not inside a building
out of fashion	:	not fashionable; not presently in common use
out of hand	:	not under control
out of harm's way	:	safe
out of line with	:	in disagreement with
be **out of** one's mind	:	be insane
out of order	:	not functioning properly; (at a formal meeting) not behaving according to the rules
out of the ordinary	:	unusual
out of place	:	unsuitable
out of practice	:	unable to do something as well as one has in past, because of lack of recent practice
out of print	:	(of a book) no longer available from the publisher
out of proportion	:	too big or too small; not having the appropriate relationship to something
out of question	:	impossible; not to be considered
out of season	:	(of fruit or vegetables) not readily available at that time of year

out of shape	:	(of persons) not in fit condition because of lack of exercise
out of sight	:	hidden, not able to be seen
out of stock	:	(of goods at a store) temporarily unavailable
out of style	:	not fashionable
out of touch	:	not in communication with; not informed about
out of town	:	having temporarily left town
out of trouble	:	not in trouble anymore
out of tune	:	not at the correct pitch
out of work	:	no longer having employment

To

to all intents and purposes	:	in all important ways
to a certain extent	:	partly
to date	:	so far; until now
up **to** date	:	current; modern
see eye **to** eye with	:	agree entirely with
take something **to** heart	:	be much affected by something
made **to** measure	:	exactly suitable; (of clothes) made for a certain person
keep something **to** oneself	:	not tell anyone
to the point	:	relevant

Under

under age	:	below the age of being legally permitted to do something
be **under** arrest	:	be held prisoner and charged with wrong doing
under the auspices of	:	with the patronage of; supported by
under one's breath	:	in a whisper
under the circumstances	:	because this is true

under consideration	:	being thought about
under control	:	able to be regulated or guided
under cover of	:	protected by; undetected because of
under fire	:	being shot at; being criticized
under the impression that	:	having the idea that
be **under** the influence of	:	be affected by
be **under** oath	:	having been sworn to tell the truth
under observation	:	being watched carefully
under restraint	:	prevented from doing something

Up

have something **up** one's sleeve	:	have a secret idea or plan in reserve

With

with impunity	:	without risk of injury or punishment
with the naked eye	:	without using a magnifying lens
with no strings attached	:	(of help given) with no conditions; to be used freely
take **with** a pinch of salt	:	not believe completely
with regard to	:	concerning; about
with respect to	:	concerning; about
tarred **with** the same brush	:	having the same faults
with a vengeance	:	very much; more than usual effort

Within

within limits	:	to a certain extent; not too much
within living memory	:	within the memory of people now alive

Without

go **without** saying	:	be obvious

Unnecessary Prepositions

In everyday speech, we fall into some bad habits; *e.g.*—using prepositions where they are not required. It would be a good idea to eliminate these words altogether, but we must be especially careful, not to use them in formal, as well as in academic prose:

1. She met ~~up with~~ the new coach on the ground.
2. The glass fell off ~~of~~ the desk.
3. He threw the glass out ~~of~~ the window.
4. He wouldn't let the cat inside ~~of~~ the house. [or use "in"]
5. Where did they go ~~to~~?
6. Where is your college ~~at~~?

Ellipsis in Preposition

When two words or phrases are used in parallel and require the same preposition in order to be idiomatically correct, the preposition does not have to be used twice. For example:

(1) You can wear that outfit *in* summer and ~~in~~ winter.

(2) The female was both attracted ~~by~~ and distracted by the male's dance.

However, when the idiomatic use of phrases calls for different prepositions, we must be careful not to omit any one of them. For example:

1. The children were *interested in* and *disgusted by* the movie.
2. It was clear that this player could both *contribute to* and *learn from* every game he played.
3. He was *fascinated by* and *enamoured of* this beguiling woman.

See some more examples:

1. We should prevent damage and theft of public property. —*Incorrect*

   We should prevent damage to and theft of public property. —*Correct*

2. He is neither ashamed nor sorry for his misdeeds. —*Incorrect*

   He is neither ashamed of nor sorry for his smisdeeds. —*Correct*

3. The design of this house is different and inferior to that of other house. —*Incorrect*

   The design of this house is different from and inferior to that of the other house. —*Correct*

Preposition Gerund

It should be understood well that verbs placed immediately after preposition must be in gerund form :

1. He prevented me from drinking cold water.
2. He insists on trying again.
3. He was debarred from taking the examination.
4. He succeeded in achieving his goal.
5. They are afraid of losing the match.
6. Ram is angry about walking in the rain.
7. Prakash is good at working in the garden.
8. I'm worried about making mistakes.
9. This girl is crazy about playing tennis.
10. He is disappointed about seeing such a bad report.
11. We are excited about making our own film.
12. Sunder is famous for singing songs.
13. I'm fed up with being treated as a child.
14. Hina is fond of going to parties.
15. She is glad about getting married again.
16. The children are not happy about seeing a doctor.
17. Are you interested in writing poems?
18. Joe is keen on drawing.
19. She is proud of riding a snowboard.
20. We're sick of sitting around like this.
21. He's sorry for eating in the classroom.
22. I'm tired of waiting you.
23. She is used to smoking.
24. He is clever at skating.

Preposition Omitted

1. Some transitive verbs do not take prepositions with them. Such commonly used verbs are; **Reach, Resist, Resemble, Afford, Accompany, Attack, Assist, Pick, Pervade, Precede, Obey, Order, Combat, Benefit, Inform, Violate,** etc.:

   (i) He ordered for a cup of tea. —*Incorrect*
   He ordered a cup of tea. —*Correct*

   (ii) India attacked on Pakistan. —*Incorrect*
   India attacked Pakistan. —*Correct*

   (iii) He informed to me yesterday. —*Incorrect*
   He informed me yesterday. —*Correct*

2. Nouns denoting time (morning, evening, day, night, month, week, year) if preceded by objective like; **this, that, next, every, last** etc., do not require preposition:

   (i) She is going to Jaipur next morning.

   (ii) I met her last evening.

   (iii) Ram is coming here next month.

3. Nouns; **Yesterday, today, tomorrow** are also used without preposition:

   (i) Please meet me tomorrow.

   (ii) He is arriving today.

   (iii) He went yesterday.

4. Words denoting time and place, like; **last week, last month, abroad, minute, bit, inside, outside,** etc., are also used without preposition:

   (i) He came here last month.

   (ii) Sita is going abroad next week.

   (iii) Please wait a minute/bit.

   (iv) Please come inside.

   (v) Why are you standing outside?

5. If verbs showing movement, like; **go, get,** etc., are used with the word 'home', we should not use any preposition before 'home':

(i) It took them three hours to get home.

(ii) I went home by bus.

Note: *If any pronoun/adjective/phrase is used immediately before 'home', the use of preposition is necessary:*

(i) She returned to her husband's home.

(ii) I went to his home.

The preposition 'at' is also used with home in the following manner:

(i) You can do this work at home.

(ii) We can stay at home.

(iii) He is at home.

Note: *We can't use **in** immediately before home.*

(i) You can do this job in your own home.

(ii) We can live in our home.

(iii) He is ***in*** home. ***Incorrect.***

6. Verbs denoting; command, request, invitation and advice, *e.g.;* **advise, ask, beg, command, encourage, implore, invite, order, recommend, remind, request, tell, urge, warn,** can be followed directly by the person addressed without the use of preposition 'to'.

Look at the following examples :

(i) I **advised her to** wait.

(ii) We **urged him to** try again.

(iii) I **reminded them** that there were no trains after 8 pm.

(iv) She **warned him** that the ice was thin.

But note that **recommend** (means advise), when used with other constructions, needs **'to'** before the person addressed :

(i) He **recommended** me to buy it.

(ii) He **recommended** it to me. (In this construction, 'to' is required)

(iii) He **recommended** me. (It would mean that he said I was suitable.)

When **'ask'** is used in the following construction, preposition **'to'** is never used after **'ask'** :

(i) He asked (me) about his health.
(ii) He asked (me) if I liked that job.
(iii) She asked (her employer) for an hour leave.

Note: *'to' is not used after **ask** in above constructions.*

Prepositions and Adverbs

Many words can be used as either prepositions or adverbs. A word functions as a preposition when it governs a noun or pronoun. When a word does not govern a noun or pronoun, it is an adverb :

(1) He was here before seven. (preposition)
(2) He has done this kind of work before. (adverb)
(3) Ramesh is behind us. (preposition)
(4) He's a long way behind. (adverb)
(5) He ran up the stairs. (preposition)
(6) He went up in the lift. (adverb)
(7) He has been ill since Monday. (preposition)
(8) I haven't seen her since. (adverb)

Verb + Preposition

A

account for : He accounted for such problems.
accuse someone of something : He accused her of stealing the money.
adapt to : They adapted to the new culture.
add someone/ something to someone/something : She added milk to the grocery list.
add to : Translation problems added to the confusion.
adjust to : They adjusted to their new environment.
admit something to someone : She admitted her real age to everybody.

admit to : She admitted to cheating on the test.

agree on : We agreed on the price.

agree to : He agreed to the new conditions.

agree with : I agree with you.

apologize to someone for something : I apologized to her for being rude.

appeal to someone for something : The nation appealed to the UN for assistance.

approve of : The parents approved of the marriage.

argue with someone about someone/ something : Timmy argued with his father about the restrictions on him.

argue with someone over something : The customer argued with the salesman over the store's return policy.

arrange for someone (to do something) : They arranged for an interpreter to be present.

arrest someone for something : The police arrested the man for stealing the car.

arrive at (a place) : They arrived at home.

ask for : She asked for help.

B

base on : The company bases the salary on experience.

be absent from (a place) : He was absent from the class.

be accustomed to : I am not accustomed to such behaviour.

be acquainted with : He is acquainted with many celebrities.

be addicted to something : He is addicted to heroin.

be afraid of : I am afraid of spiders.

be angry at someone for something : I am angry at him for what he said.

be angry with someone for something : I am angry with him for what he said.

be annoyed at someone for something : He is annoyed at her for spending so much money.

be annoyed with someone for something : He is annoyed with her for spending so much money.

be anxious about something : I am anxious about the presentation.

be associated with : He is associated with the company.

be aware of : You are not aware of all the problems.

be blessed with : He is blessed with great musical talent.

be bored by : They were bored to death by his long speech.

be bored with : The interviewers were bored with the repetitive comments.

be capable of something : He is capable of much more.

be cluttered with something : The room is cluttered with boxes.

be committed to : I am committed to improving my language skills.

be composed of : The meteorite is composed mostly of iron.

be concerned about : I am concerned about his smoking.

be connected to : The DVD player is connected to the TV.

be connected with : They are connected with the project.

be content with : He is content with the results.

be convinced of something : We are convinced of her innocence.

be coordinated with something : Testing centres coordinated with the schools to set testing dates.

be crowded in (a building or room) : It is crowded in the auditorium.

be crowded with (people) : The auditorium is crowded with people.

be dedicated to	:	She is dedicated to improving her grammatical skills.
be devoted to	:	He is devoted to his wife.
be disappointed in	:	She is disappointed in her son's improvement.
be disappointed with	:	She is disappointed with her son for not improving.
be discouraged by	:	He was discouraged by the high costs.
be discouraged from (doing something)	:	They were discouraged from participating.
be discriminated against	:	He discriminates against people who are different.
be divorced from someone	:	Mary is divorced from John.
be done with something	:	He is done with the work.
be dressed in	:	She was dressed in red.
be encouraged with	:	The staff was encouraged with a profit-sharing program.
be engaged in something	:	He was engaged in that research for more than ten years.
be engaged to someone	:	John was engaged to Mary for six months.
be envious of	:	I am envious of you for having the opportunity to travel.
be equipped with something	:	The expedition is equipped with the latest gear.
be excited about	:	I am excited about the opportunities.
be exposed to	:	The workers were exposed to dangerous chemicals.
be faced with	:	He was faced with many difficult decisions.
be faithful to	:	They are faithful to their company.
be familiar with	:	I am familiar with that programme.
be famous for	:	He is famous for climbing Mt. Everest.

be filled with : The boxes are filled with clothes and books.

be finished with : I am finished with my studies.

be fond of : She is fond of her nieces and nephews.

be friendly to someone : He is friendly to new co-workers.

be friendly with someone : He is friendly with new co-workers.

be frightened by : She is frightened by the coyotes calling at night.

be frightened of : The kids are frightened of ghosts.

be furnished with something : The house is furnished with designer furniture.

be grateful to someone for something : I am grateful to you for your assistance.

be guilty of something : He is guilty of the crime.

be happy about something : I am not happy about the results.

be innocent of something : He is innocent of the crimes.

be interested in : I am interested in astronomy.

be involved in something : He is involved in the programme.

be involved with : He is involved with many charities.

be jealous of : John is jealous of Mary's close friendship with Tom.

be known for something : He is known for his humor.

be limited to : The speeches are limited to fifteen minutes each.

be made from something : The statue is made from old car parts.

be made of (material)	:	The statue is made of metal.
be married to	:	She is married to a famous politician.
be opposed to	:	I am opposed to increasing tuition prices.
be patient with someone	:	He is patient with his students.
be pleased with	:	I am pleased with the results.
be polite to someone	:	She is polite to the visitors.
be prepared for	:	He is prepared for such questions at the conference.
be protected from	:	The cave paintings are protected from vandalism.
be proud of	:	He is proud of his son.
be related to	:	She is related to the famous artist.
be relevant to	:	That is not relevant to this conversation.
be remembered for something	:	He is remembered for his bravery.
be responsible for	:	She is responsible for the new policies.
be satisfied with	:	The teacher is satisfied with the test results.
be scared of	:	She is scared of snakes.
be terrified of	:	She is terrified of roaches.
be thankful for	:	We are thankful for their help.
be tired from (doing something)	:	He is so tired from jogging.
be tired of (doing something)	:	He is tired of answering the same questions over and over.
be worried about	:	I am worried about her.
beg for	:	They begged for the answer to the riddle.
begin with	:	Every sentence begins with a capital letter.
believe in	:	He believes in ghosts.
belong to	:	I don't belong to that organization.

benefit from	:	He benefits from the government's assistance programs.
blame someone for something	:	He blamed his employees for his mistakes.
blame something on someone	:	He blamed the company's failure on his employees.
boast about	:	She boasted about her new Mercedes.
borrow something from someone	:	He borrowed money from me.

C

care about	:	He cares about what his children watch on TV.
care for	:	He doesn't care for animals.
catch up with	:	He caught up with her before she got into the elevator.
cater to	:	The hotel doesn't cater to tour groups.
charge someone for something	:	The restaurant didn't charge me for breaking the glass.
charge someone with something	:	The police charged him with drunken driving.
choose between someone/something and someone/ something	:	The winner got to choose between a vacation to Tahiti and a new car.
choose something from something	:	The magician chose a lady from the audience to help him with the trick.
collide with	:	The car collided with a truck.
come from	:	He comes from Florida.
comment on	:	She wouldn't comment on the accusations.
communicate with someone	:	Many people use e-mail to communicate with friends and family abroad.

compare someone/ something to someone /something	The analyst compared the company's current profits to last year's.
compare someone/ something with someone/something	He shouldn't compare his younger son with his elder son.
compete with	He loves to compete with others.
complain about	They complained about the quality of the hotel.
compliment someone on something	He complimented her on her new dress.
concentrate on	He needs to concentrate on his work.
concern someone with something	You shouldn't concern her with our problems.
confess to	He confessed to the crimes.
confuse someone/ something with someone/something	She confused him with Tom Cruise.
congratulate someone on something	She congratulated him on his victory.
consent to something	The parents consented to the request.
consist of	The test consists of 100 multiple choice questions.
contribute to something	I contributed to the World Wildlife Fund.
convict someone of something	They convicted him of murder.
cope with	Can she cope with the large amount of work?
correspond with someone	I correspond with them by e-mail.
count on	He counts on their support.
cover with	She covered her sleeping son with the blanket.
crash into	He crashed into the tree.
cure someone of something	The doctors cured her of the disease.

D

deal with	:	He has to deal with many problems.
decide against	:	He decided against taking the job in New York.
decide between someone/something and someone/ something	:	I couldn't decide between the chicken dinner and the sushi.
decide on	:	He decided on taking the job in Los Angeles.
dedicate something to someone	:	He dedicated the song to his girlfriend.
demand something from someone	:	He demanded help from his co-workers.
depend on	:	The cost of the carpet depends on the quality of the weaving.
derive something from something	:	He derives a great deal of pleasure from his work.
deter someone from something	:	Nothing could deter her from becoming a police officer.
devote something to someone	:	He devoted the song to his wife.
differ from	:	Your results differ little from mine.
disagree with	:	He disagrees with me.
disapprove of	:	Her parents disapprove of her choice of the job.
discourage someone from something	:	He discouraged his son from quitting the school.
discuss something with someone	:	I discussed the situation with them.
distinguish between someone/something and someone/ something	:	The expert couldn't distinguish between the real painting and the forgery.
distract someone from something	:	The loud music distracted her from her work.

dream about	:	I dream about travelling around the world.
dream of	:	I dream of a day when poverty will no longer exist.
dress someone in something	:	She dresses her twins in similar clothes.
drink to	:	They drank to his new job.

E

elaborate on something	:	He elaborated on his earlier comments.
emerge from something	:	The dragon emerged from its lair.
escape from (a place)	:	They escaped from jail.
exchange someone/ something for someone/something	:	They exchanged dollars for yen.
exclude someone from something	:	He excluded them from the meeting.
excuse someone for something	:	She excused them for being late.
expel someone from (a place)	:	The leader was expelled from the country.
experiment on	:	They experimented on various ways of preventing the disease.
explain something to someone	:	The teacher explained the project to the students.

F

feel about	:	He felt bad about what he said.
feel like	:	I feel like seeing a movie.
fight about	:	They fought about who had to do the dishes.
fight against	:	Martin Luther King fought against racism and oppression.
fight for	:	He fought for improved working conditions.

fight with	:	He fought with his parents throughout his teen years.
forget about	:	She forgot about the meeting.
forgive someone for something	:	She forgave him for the terrible things he said.

G

gamble on	:	I wouldn't gamble on that happening.
gawk at	:	They just gawked at me as though they didn't understand a thing.
gaze at	:	She gazed at the sight in wonder.
get back from (a place)		He got back from work at 6 o'clock.
get married to someone	:	John got married to Mary.
get rid of	:	He got rid of his old clothes.
get through with	:	I'm never going to get through with this work.
get tired of	:	He got tired of complaining.
get used to	:	He needs to get used to the new working conditions.
give something to someone	:	He gave the book to me.
glare at	:	She glared at him in disbelief.
gloat at	:	He gloated at their failure.
grieve for	:	The nation is grieving for those who died in the accident.
gripe at someone	:	She always gripes at her husband.
grumble at someone about something	:	The old man always grumbles at his wife about their children never visiting them.

H

happen to	:	What happened to him?
harp on	:	She is constantly harping on her husband's bad eating habits.

hear about : I have never heard about that policy before.

hear from someone : Have you heard from your son recently?

hear of : Have you ever heard of the Anasazi people?

help someone with something : He helped me with my homework.

hide something from someone : He hid his bad report card from his parents.

hinder someone/ something from something : Rebels are hindering aid workers from accessing the area.

hinge on : Success hinges on his participation in the project.

hope for : The company hopes for better sales in the coming quarter.

I

insist on : He insists on driving even though he is having vision problems.

insure against : The investment does not insure against loss of income.

interfere in something: The couple's parents should not interfere in their relationship.

interfere with something : Don't interfere with the delicate balance of nature.

introduce someone/ something to someone/something : I introduced him to my girlfriend.

invest in : We invested in that company.

invite someone to : I invited her to the party.

involve someone/ something in something : We involved them in the decision-making.

J

jabber about	:	He was jabbering <u>about</u> problems at work.
joke about	:	We love to sit around and joke <u>about</u> old times.
joke with someone about someone/ something	:	He was joking <u>with</u> me about the mistake I made.
jot down something	:	She jotted <u>down</u> notes as he spoke.

K

keep on (doing something)	:	She kept <u>on</u> talking.
keep someone/ something from (doing something)	:	I kept her <u>from</u> making the same mistake.
keep something for someone	:	He wants to keep the toy <u>for</u> his daughter.
know about	:	He knows a lot <u>about</u> that subject.

L

laugh about	:	She laughed <u>about</u> what the children had done.
laugh at	:	We always laugh <u>at</u> his jokes.
learn about	:	I need to learn more <u>about</u> that topic.
lend something to someone	:	I lent my dictionary <u>to</u> her.
listen for	:	The mechanic said I should listen <u>for</u> any squeaking sounds.
listen to	:	He loves <u>to</u> listen to his MP3 player on the subway.
long for	:	I long <u>for</u> a week on the beach in Hawaii.
look at	:	Look <u>at</u> this old picture of my grandmother.
look forward to	:	I look forward <u>to</u> meeting her parents.

meet with someone : We will meet with the organizers next week.

mistake someone/ something for someone/something : I mistook him for his twin brother; I mistook the curd for the milk.

N

nod at : He nodded at the others.

nod to : He nodded to them.

O

object to : Do you object to my smoking?

operate on : The surgeon operated on the conjoined twins.

P

participate in something : We participated in the survey.

pay for : He paid for our meal last night.

persist in : The disease persists in rural farms throughout the region.

plan on : We plan on attending the wedding.

praise someone for something : He praises his son for his good grades.

pray for : The villagers prayed for rain.

prefer someone/ something to someone/something : We prefer salmon to other kinds of fish; For partnership, he prefers Ram to Raju.

prepare for : We are preparing for a long winter.

present someone with something : He will present her with the award for best journalist.

prevent someone/ something from (doing something) : The campaign is designed to prevent young people from drinking.

prohibit someone from: (doing something): The school prohibits students from smoking.

provide for : It is difficult for them to provide for their families.

provide someone with something : The school provides students with textbooks.

provide someone/ something for someone : The company will provide food and drinks for all.

punish someone for something : He was punished for his crimes.

Q

quarrel with someone about something : They quarrelled with the waiter about the mistakes in the bill.

quarrel with someone over something : He quarrelled with her over her political beliefs.

R

react to : He reacted to the news negatively.

recover from something : He is recovering from his illness.

refer to something : He was referring to the chart on page 24.

relate to : She is not related to their family.

rely on : We rely on the latest information to make such decisions.

remind someone of someone/something : He reminds me of my grandfather.

reply to : We replied immediately to the letter.

rescue someone from someone/something : He rescued the puppy from the icy lake.

resign from something: He resigned from the company.

respond to : We responded to the request for help.

result in something : His outburst resulted in his being fired.

retire from something : He retired from the company after 40 years of faithful service.

S

save someone from something	: They are working to save mountain gorillas from extinction.
search for	: They are searching for signs of life on Mars.
sentence someone to something	: The court sentenced him to 20 years in jail.
separate someone/ something from someone/something	: He separated Billy from the other children.
share something with someone	: She shared her secret with others.
shout at	: The old man shouted at the noisy kids.
show something to someone	: He showed the pictures to his friends.
smile at someone	: I smiled at the newcomers.
speak to someone about someone/ something	: The director spoke to the employees about the changes.
specialize in something	: He specializes in technical translation.
spend (money/time) **on**	: They spent too much money on their new car.
stand for	: NASA stands for National Aeronautics and Space Administration.
stare at	: Why are they staring at me?
stem from	: The corruption charges stem from allegations of bribery.
stop someone from (doing something)	: The environmental group stopped them from building the new hotel.
subject someone to something	: They subject the students to unrealistic standards.

subscribe to	:	He subscribed to that magazine.
substitute someone/ something for someone/something	:	You can substitute beef for pork if you don't eat pork.
subtract something from something	:	He subtracted the expenses from the profits.
succeed at something	:	He will succeed at anything he does.
succeed in (doing something)	:	He succeeded in finishing the marathon.
suffer from	:	She suffers from a rare genetic disorder.
suspect someone of something	:	The police suspect them of smuggling drugs over the border.

T

take advantage of	:	He took advantage of his connections at the company.
take care of	:	He takes care of his pets.
talk about	:	They talked about the recent problems.
talk to	:	I need to talk to you for a few minutes.
tell someone about something	:	He told them about what had happened.
thank someone for something	:	We thanked them for their hospitality.
think about	:	He thought about what she had said.
think of	:	They need to think of ways to reduce costs.
toast to	:	Let's toast to a long marriage.
translate something into (a language)	:	He translated the instructions into Japanese.
trust someone with something	:	He trusted the new employee with a major project.
turn to	:	He turned to page 101.

U

use something for something : They use coal for fuel.

V

vote against : She voted against the new proposal.

vote for : He voted for the Congress party.

W

wait for : I waited for them at the restaurant.

warn about : They warned me about pickpockets at the railway station.

waste (money/time) **on** : They wasted money on another new car.

wish for : The child wished for a new bicycle before he blew out the candles on his cake.

work for : I have worked for them for 20 years.

work on : They worked on the proposal for two weeks.

worry about : She worries about her children.

write about : He wrote a book about his life.

write to someone : You need to write to your parents more often.

Y

yap about : He always yaps about the good old days.

yearn for : He yearns for more adventure in his life.

Using Prepositions

1. **Abide at (place) :** I will abide at the railway station till the train arrives.

   Abide in (house) : She has been abiding in my house for the last three months.

   Abide by (decision) : She will abide by my decision positively.

   Abide with (person) : He will abide with his friend Suresh in all circumstances.

2. **Angry at (thing) :** He is angry at your way of questioning.

   Angry with (person) : Sunita is angry with Raju.

   Angry for (action) : He is angry for your laughing at his wife.

3. **Arrive at (place) :** The train is going to arrive at the station within ten minutes.

   Arrive in (country) : He is scheduled to arrive in India on next Monday.

4. **Alight on (ground, thing) :** A large number of birds alight on the roof of my house.

   Alight at (a place) : The groom alighted from the elephant at the gate.

5. **Appeal to (person) :** I earnestly appealed to the principal to consider the matter again.

   Appeal against (decision) : He appealed against the decision of the lower court.

6. **Amuse at (thing) :** He is greatly amused at the indifferent attitude of his father.

   Amused with (action) : The boys amused themselves with throwing flowers at the girls.

7. **Ask for (a thing) :** He asked me for some help.

   Ask from (person) : He asked some help from me.

8. **Affiliated to (University, Board) :** Our school is affiliated to the CBSE Board.

   Affiliated with (a party) : Bajrang Dal is affiliated with the BJP indirectly.

9. **Annoyed at (thing) :** He became annoyed at my laughing.

   Annoyed with (person) : He is annoyed with you.

10. **Antipathy to (thing) :** He has a great antipathy to wine.

    Antipathy against (person) : You should not have any antipathy against your friend Jack.

11. **Answer to (person) :** You have to answer to me for your conduct.

    Answer for (action) : He was asked to answer for the misbehaviour.

12. **Arm against (danger) :** We must arm ourselves against the danger of chemical weapons.

    Arm with (weapon) : He armed himself with a revolver and a knife.

13. **Atone to (person) :** I tried to atone to him by offering market price of the land.

    Atone for (action) : He tried to atone for the mischief he had committed.

14. **Award for (action) :** He was awarded a gold medal for winning 100 metre race.

    Awarded to (person) : A silver medal will be awarded to the best sports girl.

15. **Antidote to (medicine) :** Diamond is regarded as an antidote to the poison of the snake.

    Antidote against (infection) : Quinine is an antidote against malaria.

16. **Argue against or about (a matter) :** He went to argue against the topic of debate.

    He argued well about the newly introduced bill.

    Argue with (person) : Don't argue with me unnecessarily.

17. **Agree in (opinion) :** Ganesh agrees with Ram in opinion expressed by him (Ram).

Agree to (proposal) : I cannot agree to his proposal of dividing the property.

Agree with (person) : I fully agree with you on this issue.

Agree on (subject) : After a lot of discussion, all agreed on the terms of agreement.

18. **Accomplice with (person) :** His wife was an accomplice with the murderer.

Accomplice in (act) : His wife was an accomplice in the murder.

19. **Authority for (action) :** You have no authority for instructing me as such.

Authority on (subject) : She is indeed an unquestionable authority on Physics.

Authority over (person) : He has no authority over me officially.

20. **Accused of (a crime) :** He is accused of murder.

21. **Accused by (a person) :** He was accused by his wife.

B

1. **Blush for (fault) :** She blushed for the misbehaviour of her husband.

Blush at (praise) : She blushed at the compliments showered by her husband.

2. **Blind to (deeds, action) :** He should not be blind to the misdeeds of his son Rakesh.

Blind in (one eye) : Her husband is blind in the right eye.

3. **Born of (parents) :** He was born of an orthodox mother.

Born at, in (place) : He was born at the general hospital in Alwar.

4. **Buy from (shop) :** You can buy this item from any grocery shop.

Buy for (person) : I bought this ball pen for my son.

5. **Beg of, from (person) :** I begged of him to give me some time to pay.

   I begged some rice from him.

6. **Beg for (thing) :** I begged him for some rice.

C

1. **Close to (as adjective) :** His house is very close to the railway station.

   Close with (means—to shut) : She closed the door with a bang.

   Close down (mens—to terminate the operation) : He closed down his shop within six months.

   Close out (means—to reduce the price) : He closed out the price of sugar to increase sales.

2. **Confer about (refers to consult of a matter) :** Ram and Rahim confer together about nominating the secretary.

   Confer with (refers to consult with a person) : I will confer with my father in this matter.

3. **Contend for (thing) :** S.S. Shekhawat will contend for a seat in Vidhan Sabha.

   Contend with (person) : You should not contend with a person like Lalu Singh.

4. **Consist in (means—remain) :** The beauty of this building consists in its style and grandeur.

   Consist of (means—composed of) : Our body consists of flesh, bone and blood.

5. **Condemn to (punishment) :** He was condemned to death by the judge.

   Condemn for (crime) : He was condemned for murder by the court.

6. **Compare to (comparing two different kind of things) :** Don't compare water to milk.

   Compare with (comparing two things of same class) : Kalidas was compared with Shakespeare by several renowned scholars.

7. **Care for (means—like) :** I do not care for drinks.
Care about (thing) : She takes full care about her sarees and make-up.
8. **Consult on (matter) :** We were not consulted on the new issue of debentures.
Consult with (person) : You should consult with some expert before taking a final decision.
9. **Controversy on (matter) :** A lot of controversy was raised on this issue.

   Controversy with (person) : I do not have any controversy with any of the members on this matter.
10. **Confide to (means—to tell) :** You should not confide your secrets to any body.

    Confide in (means—to pose confidence) : I confided in him, but he deceived me.
11. **Complain of (a thing) :** I complained of his misconduct to the boss.

    Complain to (person) : I complained of his misbehaviour to his father.
12. **Compete with (person) :** Can you compete with him ?

    Compete for (job) : I will try my best to compete for this job.
13. **Cause of (problem) :** He is the main cause of all this trouble.

    Cause for (anxiety) : I do not have any cause for anxiety.
14. **Clothed in (dressing) :** She was clothed in a dress.

    Clothed with (Some quality) : She was clothed with shame.
15. **Connect to (join) :** Connect the end of this rod to the other.

    Connect with (relation) : I have no connection with her for the last three years.

1. **Displeased at (thing) :** She is not displeased at such humorous jokes.

   Displeased with (person) : Raju is greatly displeased with Sunita.

2. **Disqualified for (post) :** She was declared disqualified for the election.

   Disqualified from (competing) : He was disqualified from taking part in the competition.

3. **Dwell upon (means—to speak) :** The Chairman dwelt upon the importance of truth and honesty.

   Dwell in (country) : The French dwell in France.

   Dwell at (place) : These days, Ram is dwelling at his friend's hotel.

   Dwell among (people) : He is dwelling among the tribals.

4. **Disgusted at (thing) :** She became disgusted at your silly joke.

   Disgusted with (person or life) : I am very much disgusted with him.

5. **Deal with (means—to do with the matter) :** This book deals with the population problem in India.

   Deal in (trade) : He deals in iron scrap.

   Deal out (means—to distribute) : The principal should deal out equal treatment to all the teachers.

6. **Differ on (point) :** I totally differ on this point.

   Differ with (person) : I differ with you on this point.

   Differ from (thing) : Your views differ entirely from that of mine.

7. **Die of (a disease) :** He died of hunger/cholera.

   Die from (some cause) : He died from hard labour.

8. **Destined for (means—created for) :** God had destined him for the post of President of India.

   Destined to (subject) : He is destined to such a pitiable condition.

9. **Dine with (person) :** I am scheduled to dine with him to-night.

   Dine on (thing) : I can't dine on same kind of menu daily.

10. **Dispense with (means—do with/without) :** Jack can't easily dispensen with her.

Dispense to (means—distribute) : A judge must dispense equal justice to all.

11. **Dispose of (means—to sell) :** She wants to dispose of all the goods at the earliest.

Dispose to (state of things) : The news of his father's death disposed him to a deep sorrow.

12. **Dispute with (person) :** Why are you disputing with your friends on such a trifle matter?

Dispute about (thing) : There was a great dispute about nomination of the chairman.

E

1. **Embark on (a vessel) :** She embarked on the ship for Sri-Lanka.

Embark in (new business) : He has embarked in the new business with full fervour.

2. **Enter into (thing) :** They have entered into an agreement with Ramesh.

Enter upon (new course) : After marriage, I entered upon a new way of life.

3. **Exchange for (thing) :** She exchanged the book for a piece of art.

Exchange with (person) : I want to exchange my views with you.

4. **Exult at (success) :** She was exulted at her brilliant success.

Exult over (an enemy) : Our army exulted over the enemy's force.

Exult in (misery) : One should not be exulted in the misery of others.

5. **Eager for (fame) :** She is very eager for making a name in society.

Eager in (to find) : He has involved himself eagerly in pursuit of finding the cause of miseries in life.

6. **Equivalent for (word) :** Write a word equivalent for 'fear'.

   Equivalent to (money, thing) : One million is equivalent to ten lacs.

7. **Exact from (person) :** Heavy fines were exacted from the unruly students.

   Exact in (as adjective) : He is not exact in repayment.

8. **Expert in (doing) :** He is expert in repairing automobiles.

   Expert at (thing) : He is expert at English Grammar.

9. **Enquire of (person) :** I enquired of him the secret of his happiness.

   Enquire into (a matter) : The police enquired into the case of bank robbery.

10. **Entrust with (a thing) :** I entrusted him with my camera.

    Entrust to (person) : I entrusted my camera to him.

F

1. **Fit out (means—equip) :** The ship was fitted out for Sri-Lanka.

   Fit up (means—furnishing) : He fitted up his house with all necessary furniture.

2. **Fascinated with (person) :** I was fascinated with Rekha.

   Fascinated by (thing) : I was fascinated by her manners and looks.

3. **False to (person) :** One should not be false to one's friends.

   False of (thing, heart) : He is not false of heart.

4. **Fight for (means—defend) :** Our army is ready to fight for the country.

   Fight with (together) : We must not fight with our friends.

   Fight against (thing) : We must fight against the evil of illiteracy.

5. **Familiar to (thing) :** Your looks are quite familiar to that of Sachin.

   Familiar with (person) : I am familiar with him.

G

1. **Gaze at (means—look attentively at) :** Don't gaze at these girls, they are the cops.

   Gaze on (means—look strangely) : He stood gazing on the pathetic scene of accident.

2. **Grieve for (person) :** She was extremely grieved for him.

   Grieve at (event) : Everyone was grieved at the death of Rajeev Gandhi.

   Grieve over (thing) : She was grieved over my unfortunate loss.

3. **Good for (nothing) :** He is good for nothing fellow.

   Good at (something) : She is good at swimming.

1. **Held by (person) :** A condolence meeting was held by the staff yesterday.

   Held in (esteem or contempt) : In the heart of every Indian, Gandhiji is held in great respect.

   Held at (place) : A meeting was held at Hope Circus yesterday.

2. **Hear of (something) :** I heard of this robbery from Sarla.

   Hear from (person) : I heard of this robbery from Sarla.

   Hear by (post) : I hear by this letter about your promotion.

3. **Happen to (person) :** Please tell me what happened to you in New York.

   Happen at (place) : This event happened at the Red Square.

   Happen on (means—come across) : While returning from the market, I happened on a gang of thieves.

4. **Hidden from (view) :** The neem tree has hidden your house from direct view.

   Hidden by (person, thing) : My shoes were hidden by my sister.

I

1. **Introduce to (person) :** Let me first introduce my friend to you.

   Introduce into (means—make modifications) : The UPSC has introduced many changes into the syllabus of IAS.

2. **Invest with (authority) :** The President invested him with the honour of Bharat Ratna.

   Invest in (business) : I am ready to invest Rs. fifty lacs in this business.

3. **Inquire for (a thing) :** I went there to inquire for my lost brief-case.

   Inquire into (matter) : The police will inquire into the cause of death.

   Inquire about (refers—concern) : She came here to inquire about the health of her son.

   Inquire of (refers—asking) : First inquire of the way, then move.

4. **Involve in (thing) :** She seems to be involved in some serious trouble.

   Involve with (person) : Don't involve yourself with such unruly persons.

5. **Irritated at (thing) :** I was greatly irritated at his unruly behaviour.

   Irritated against (person) : She was extremely irritated against her husband.

6. **Impatient at (unexpected thing) :** He became impatient at the unexpected delay.

   Impatient for (expected thing) : She is very impatient for the arrival of her husband.

7. **Indebted for (thing) :** I was indebted for your timely help.

   Indebted to (person) : He is greatly indebted to Rani for her timely help.

J

1. **Jest at (person) :** I don't like to jest at a lunatic person.

   Jest with (thing) : We should not jest with the communal overtones in the society.

2. **Judge of (giving opinion) :** Without going in details, how can you judge of this matter.

   Judge by (observing) : Judging by her qualifications, I think she is not fit for this job.

1. **Know by (means—recognize by) :** A man is known by his actions.

   Know for (quality) : He is known for his foolish decisions.

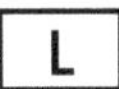

1. **Live at (a small town) :** He lives at Alwar in Rajasthan.

   Live in (in country, big place) : He is living at Alwar in Rajasthan.

   Live on (food) : He lives entirely on breads.

   Live for (means—devote) : We must live and die for the cause of truth.

   Live with (a person) : I live here with my parents.

2. **Liable for (crime) :** You are liable for the death of your wife.

   Liable to (punishment) : He was liable to imprisonment for three years.

3. **Listen for (sound) :** I am listening for the voice of Lata Mangeshkar.

   Listen to (means—hear attentively) : We should listen to the advice of our elders.

4. **Laugh at (means—make fun of) :** We must not laugh at our friends.

   Laugh with (means—indulge with) : Better to laugh with the disabled than to laugh at them.

M

5. **Married to (a woman) :** Ramesh was married to Sarla.

   Married with (a man) : Sarla was married with Ramesh.

6. **Moved with (sorrow) :** He was actually moved with a feeling of sorrow.

   Moved to (tears) : On hearing the news of sudden death of his wife, all moved to tears.

   Moved from (one's determination) : You can't move me from my decision with your logic.

   Moved at (a scene) : He was greatly moved at the sight of her mother's dead body.

1. **Obliged to (person) :** I am very much obliged to you.

   Obliged at (thing) : I am obliged for your timely help.

2. **Occupied in (doing a job) :** He is fully occupied in writing a book.

   Occupied by (thing) : That house is occupied by a marriage party.

3. **Originate with (person) :** All the planning originated with him.

   Originate in (place, cause) : A fierce fire originated in Connaught Place yesterday.

1. **Part from (person) :** I parted from my wife with a heavy heart.

   Part with (thing) : He is not ready to part with his furniture at any cost.

2. **Prepare for (means—be ready for) :** I am preparing for the IAS examination this year.

   Prepare against (danger) : We must prepare ourselves against the dangers of water pollution.

3. **Pray for (thing) :** My wife prayed for my success.

   Pray to (make prayer) : I prayed to God to help me in facing the unwarranted problems.

4. **Perish by (famine) :** Our district was perished by the drought last year.

   Perish with (hunger) : During drought, the cattle perish with starvation.

5. **Plead with (person) :** He pleaded with the principal for mercy.

   Plead for (thing) : He pleaded with the king for mercy.

6. **Play at (cards) :** They were playing at cards.

   Play upon (musical instrument) : Harish played upon the violin in the party.

1. **Quick in (doing) :** He is quick in reasoning questions .

   Quick of (understanding) : Ramesh is quick of understanding the questions.

2. **Quarrel over (thing) :** You must not quarrel over the parental property.

   Quarrel with (person) : We must not quarrel with our friends.

1. **Responsible to (person) :** An MLA is responsible to the Chief Minister.

   Responsible for (action) : She is responsible for the loss caused due to her negligence.

2. **Reason with (person) :** I reasoned with him on each and every point in this matter.

   Reason about (thing) : You can't reason about the importance of self-respect.

3. **Ready for (action) :** I am ready for the match.

Ready with (something) : I was totally ready with my arguments on that day.

Ready in (replying) : I always found her ready in her reply.

4. **Revenge on (person) :** He revenged himself on his enemy.

Revenge for (action) : I will positively revenge for the insult inflicted on me by her.

5. **Reduced to (means—to decrease to) :** His salary was reduced to rupees four thousand per month.

Reduced by (refers to decrease by an amount) : His salary was reduced by three hundred rupees per month.

S

1. **Share of (thing) :** I must be paid my share of profit.

Share with (person) : I do not share my lunch with anybody.

2. **Skilful at (thing) :** He is skilful at numbers.

Skilful in (doing a thing) : He is skilful in mathematical calculations.

3. **Succeed to (property) :** He succeeded to his uncle's empire.

Succeed in (doing) : This time she succeeded in IAS examination.

4. **Start at (time) :** I started at 10 o'clock in the morning.

Start from (place) : I start at 10 o'clock in the morning from Delhi.

Started for (place) : I started at 7 o'clock in the morning for Delhi.

5. **Struggle for (thing) :** We have to struggle hard for keeping peace in the country.

Struggle with (person) : We should not struggle with our neighbours.

6. **Serve out (means—to distribute) :** Sweets were served out to the audience.

Serve up (means—to give food) : A nice lunch was served up there in the function.

7. **Speak for (person) :** You go there, I have already spoken for you to the secretary.

   Speak about (thing) : He is speaking about the 'unemployment problem'.

8. **Starved to (death) :** She was starved to death by her husband.

   Starved with (hunger) : He starved with hunger.

9. **Suited for (action) :** She is not suited for the role of vamp.

   Suited to (occasion) : The song suited to the occasion.

10. **Supply to (person) :** PHED is supplying water to all the colonies in the city.

    Supply with (thing) : Government must supply the poor with food and clothing.

T

1. **Thankful for (thing) :** I am really thankful for your timely help.

   Thankful to (person) : I am very thankful to you for your kind favour.

2. **Think over (means—to consider) :** The society agreed to think over the case in the next meeting.

   Think on (means—meditate) : I have been thinking on this matter for the last many days.

3. **Trust in (person) :** Trust in God and work hard.

   Trust to (thing) : I trusted to his words and he was right.

4. **Tired of (means—disgusted) :** I am tired of your daily excuses.

   Tired with (means—exhausted) : You seem to be tired with the long run.

5. **Talk with (person) :** I will talk with my father on this matter.

   Talk about (thing) : I will talk about this matter with my parents.

   Talk over (means—to discuss) : All the members of the society talked over the issue for many hours.

U

1. **Useful for (thing) :** The bag is very useful for picnic parties.
   Useful to (person) : I find that these directives are useful to me for success in the exam.

1. **Vote for (person) :** Vote for me, please.

   Vote on (a resolution) : After having cast votes on the resolution, all took lunch.
2. **Vexed with (person) :** Why are you vexed with your wife?

   Vexed at (thing) : He is vexed at my jokes.

1. **Wait at (place) :** I will wait at the church near the hospital.

   Wait for (person) : I will wait for you up to tomorrow.
2. **Wake up (means—to get up) :** She wakes up at 6 am daily.

   Wake from (means—to be awaken) : She waked from slumber and decided to take action.
3. **Warn against (an action) :** I have already warned you against such negligence.

   Warn of (danger) : I have already warned you of the risk involved.

Z

1. **Zealous for (a thing) :** A dedicated worker is always zealous for achieving the target.

   Zealous in (a cause) : We must be zealous in the cause of humanity.

Appropriate Prepositions

This section is about appropriate prepositions following certain nouns, verbs, adjectives, and adverbs.

Idioms call for certain nouns, verbs, adjectives and adverbs to be followed by particular prepositions. Some of such commonly used cases are listed below:

abundance of	(wealth)
assent to	(a proposal)
accustomed to	(work)
avail ourselves of	(an opportunity)
attain to	(a position)
addicted to	(drinking, etc.)
accede to	(a request)
abstain from	(food, indulgence etc.)
absolved from	(a promise, a sin)
acquiesce in	(an opinion, in proposal)
adhere to	(principles)
afraid of	(a ghost)
abhorrent to	(good nature)
accession to	(throne)
assure of	(a thing)
absorbed in	(study)
acquit	(someone of a charge)
acquaintance with	(a person)
accord with	(*but*, of one's own accord)
account for	
adverse to	
agree on	(terms)
agree to	(a proposal)
agree with	(a person)

aim at	
alien to	
averse to	(*not* averse from)
aware of	
begin by	(doing something)
begin from	(a point)
begin with	(an act)
benefits of	(the benefactor)
benefits to	(the beneficiary)
capable of	
capacity for	
circumstances	(in the)
compare with	(to note the points of resemblance and difference)
compare to	(only when used in the sense—'to liken to')
concur with	(a person)
conditions	(under the)
conform to	(means—adapt one's self to)
conform with	(means—in harmony with)
consist in	(definition; Memory consists in a present imagination of past incidents.)
consist of	(material; The meal consisted of fish.)
consistent with	
content oneself with	
content others by	
contrast	(When *contrast* is used as a verb, it is followed by *with*. Either *to* or *with* may be used when the word *contrast* is used as a noun.)
conversant with	
correspond to	(means—resemble)

correspond with	(means—communicate)
comply with	(one's wishes)
condemn to	(death)
cured of	(a disease)
conducive to	(health)
demand for	(a thing)
demand (a thing) from	(a person)
demand of	(a person)
derive from	
differ, different from	(*not* than or to)
differ with	(a person, in opinion)
disagree with	(a person)
despair of	(success)
desirous of	(doing something)
deprive of	(something)
devoid of	(quality)
duty of	(the country)
eligible for	(a post)
embark	(in a mining venture/embark on a journey)
endowed with	
evidence of	(something)
evidence for	(a theory)
exception to	(a rule)
excuse for	(a fault)
envious of	(a person or a thing)
exchange a thing	(with a person)
elder to	(some family member)
find a fault in	(a person or thing)
find fault with	(a person)
free from	

fatal to	(one's cause)
fearful of	(death)
furnish with	(clothes)
greedy of	(money)
heir to	(ancestral property)
healed of	(a disease)
hopeful of	(success)
hostile to	(a person)
hunger after	(fame)
innocent of	(a crime)
intimate with	(a person)
invite to	(dinner)
insist on	(a thing)
intimate with	(a person)
impertinent to	(elders)
insight into	(a matter or thing)
indifferent to	
infected with	(a disease, bad qualities)
infested with	(insects, vermin)
initiative in	(to take on one's own initiative)
insight into	
interpreted as	(avoid 'interpreted to be', as this implies cause and effect)
invest in	(a business)
jealous of	(a person)
join in	(a project)
join with	(a person or thing)
key to	(success)
keep to	(the left, the point)
knock at	(the door)

labour at	(a task)
labour for	(a person, an end)
labour in	(a good cause)
labour under	(a disadvantage)
look after	(a business)
look at	(a thing)
look for	(a missing article)
look into	(a matter)
look over	(an account)
match for	(a person)
mourn for	(the dead)
mad with	(anger)
motive for	(an action)
on the spur of the	(moment)
at a moment's notice	(at a)
need for	(help)
need of	(a thing)
notorious for	(drinking, etc.)
order of	(in the)
occur to	(mind)
overwhelmed with	(sorrow, grief)
parallel with or to	
perpendicular to	
point at	(a thing)
point to	(a fact)
point with	(an object)
prefer one to	(the other)
prefer to	(do one thing rather than another)
preference for	
prevent from	(doing something)

proceed to	(an act not previously started)
proceed with	(an act already started)
prohibit	(from doing something)
provide against	(ill luck)
provide for	(an emergency)
provide **oneself** with	(something)
pursuant to	(means—in pursuance of)
pay for	(one's mistakes)
passion	(for study)
peculiar to	(a person or a thing)
persist in	(doing)
pity for	(the poor, downtrodden)
pleased with	(a person)
preface to	(a book)
proud of	(a thing)
pride on	(a thing)
range from	(x to y, *not* range between)
ready to	(do something)
ready with	(a reply)
reckon with	(a person, a contingency)
reference to	(preceded by *with*, not *in*)
regard for a person	(with regard *to* a *subject*)
regard for	(one's own interest)
relief to suffering	(preceded by to bring)
relieve one from	(a duty)
responsibility for	(an act or situation)
responsibility of	(deciding, of a position)
responsibility to	(a person for an action)
result from	(an event)

result in	(a failure)
result of	(an investigation)
right of	(doing something)
right to	(do)
refrain from	(doing something wrong)
repent of	(a mistake)
respectful to	(a person)
rob a person of	(a thing)
satisfied of	(a fact)
satisfied with	(a thing)
secure against	(an attack)
secure from	(harm)
secure in	(a position)
sentence to	(punishment)
short of	(money)
side with	(a person)
shocked at	(a loss)
superior to	(a thing)
sure of	(some fact)
search for	(a thing)
sacred to	(a cause)
surrender to	(an enemy, authority)
stick to	(a point)
suspect of	(something)
translate into	
touch upon	(subject)
slur on	(character)
tamper with	(evidence)
tinker at	(gemmology)

tinker with	(an engine)
triumph over	(difficulties)
troubles to	(person)
unconscious of	
(at) variance on	(certain topics)
(at) variance with	(a person)
versed in	
(in) view of	(circumstances)
view to a purpose	(preceded by—with a)
vain of	(beauty)
wary of	(a danger)
want of	(money)
wanting in	(wisdom)
worthy of	(a reward)
yield to	(an enemy)

EXERCISES

Exercise 1

Fill in the blanks with the most appropriate preposition chosen from those given in brackets :

1. This train travels from New Delhi .... Bhubaneshwar. (at, to)
2. We stood at the back .... the building. (of, on)
3. She went to Mumbai .... Delhi. (versus, via)
4. The store is open daily ....Monday to Friday. (for, from)
5. I took my hat .... the table. (of, off)
6. He looks ....his brother. (despite, like)
7. The children ran .... the school. (of, out of)
8. He opened the box .... a screwdriver. (at, with)
9. I will work .... five o'clock. (until, up)
10. We walked ....the restaurant. (despite, past)
11. At three o'clock, we reached the top .... the hill. (of, off)
12. You have delivered all the papers .... this one. (between, but)
13. The bank is ....the school. (opposite, out of)
14. .... the danger, he decided to climb the mountain. (despite, except)
15. The treasure was hidden .... the earth. (under, upto)
16. 'A' comes .... 'B' in the alphabet. (before, behind)
17. I went to work .... my bag. (out of, without)
18. When heated, ice changes ....water. (in, into)
19. Nocturnal animals usually sleep.........the day. (during, underneath)
20. The squirrel ran .... the wall. (along, among)
21. She made a speech .... the future of the school. (about, around)
22. 'D' comes .... 'C' and 'E' in the alphabet. (between, beyond)

Exercise 2

Fill in blanks appropriately with the following prepositions:
[for, to, at, in, with, from, against, into, after, towards, along, on]

1. Containing all of his works, this collection includes many things which are published..........the first time.
2. Dean is sitting in his cell.......... Death Row in San Quentin Prison.
3. If it does not sound like a big deal.........you, maybe you would feel different if it were you on trial.
4. The design of the courtroom puts the defendent ......a disadvantage when he goes to trial.
5. This set up seems to make the person ...... trial distant, and not even a real part of the proceedings.
6. If a juror states that he opposes the death penalty, he will be excused .... serving on the jury.
7. It is not unusual .... visitors to wait for an hour or longer.
8. There is a strong contingent of pro-death jurors sitting ......the jury pool.
9. This process tends to heavily slant the jury pool .....those jurors who are supportive of the death penalty.
10. He appeared in front of the jury .... handcuffs and dressed in a white apparel.
11. Bamboo is the fastest growing plant ......this planet.
12. Everyday, I went to the yard, I would lean ....the wall.
13. Bamboo provided the first re-greening in Hiroshima ......the atomic blast in 1945.
14. The anti-erosion properties of bamboo create an effective watershed, binding the soil together ...... the fragile river banks.
15. His dialogue is precise and tailored ...... the neurotic contours of individual characters.
16. Lawrence was a masterful and lyrical writer, whose story takes us bodily ...... the world of its characters.
17. Those short stories celebrate the vitality that is fundamental ......Lawrence's vision of life.

18. "Women Chorus" examines the ill effects of industrialization ...... the human psyche.
19. Her interest ......and fascination......the writings of Tagore is everywhere manifested in her manuscript.
20. I highly recommend this book to all readers who wish to gain insight ......children psychology.

Exercise 3

Fill in the blanks with the correct prepositions chosen from the pairs given in brackets :

1. Heat and light radiate ....the sun. (from, of)
2. Where the event will be held depends .... the weather. (of, on)
3. She loves to quote.........Shakespeare's plays. (from, to)
4. You need to concentrate ....what you are doing. (into, on)
5. The students protested .... the high tution fees. (against, from)
6. A balanced meal consists .... vitamins, minerals, proteins and carbohydrates. (of, with)
7. Twenty people applied .... the job. (for, with)
8. She likes to participate .... extra-curricular activities. (in, with)
9. He paid .... the meal. (for, on)
10. We do not approve ....that type of behaviour. (of, in)
11. He subscribes ....four magazines. (of, to)
12. The dog barked .... the mailman. (at, to)
13. Please refrain ....smoking. (from, to)
14. Do you concur ....my conclusions? (for, with)
15. The problem stems .... a lack of proper training. (for, from)
16. We apologized .... our absence. (for, to)
17. He is engaged .... starting a business. (in, on)
18. The two children stared .... each other. (at, to)
19. They registered.........the course. (for, of)
20. We rely .... the city bus service. (on, with)
21. He likes listcning .... music. (on, to)
22. They cooperated ....one another. (of, with)

Exercise 4

Fill in the blanks with appropriate prepositions:

1. Ram killed the snake .... a stick.
2. He lives .... Alwar.
3. Rice is selling .... five rupees a kilo.
4. His car ran .... a dog.
5. He assured to stand .... me in all circumstances.
6. I will stand .... for my rights.
7. He put .... a coat of red colour.
8. He is proud .... his riches.
9. He lives .... Mumbai.
10. In general, acids act .... metals.
11. Raju was beaten .... by Mohan for no reason.
12. He sat .... the ground.
13. He felled the tree .... an axe.
14. An epidemic broke .... in the town last year.
15. I called .... to her from a distant place.

Exercise 5

Fill in the blanks with appropriate prepositions :

1. He finished the work .... four hours.
2. I took him .... a thief.
3. Mahesh is now rid .... all his troubles.
4. He sat .... me.
5. He agreed .... my plan.
6. The cat ran .... the mouse.
7. He died .... heart failure.
8. He fell .... the bed.
9. They were walking .... the road.
10. He rushed .... the pathway.
11. He acted according .... my desire.
12. We did it ....you.

13. Anil goes to office .... car.
14. Look .... the picture.
15. He ran .... the room and sat .... his father.

Exercise 6

Correct the following sentences :

1. You cannot prevent me to go to the market.
2. She refrains to do this work.
3. I insisted him to attend the class.
4. He has a passion to learn English grammar.
5. She is negligent to attend the meetings.
6. She persisted to write again.
7. He is bent to fight again.
8. I am confident to win the match.
9. He succeeded to pass the examination this time.
10. I am proud to have a friend like Ram.
11. I cannot hinder her to enter the temple.
12. She is desirous to leave the place.
13. Raju was disqualified to compete in this tournament.
14. I cannot think to oppose him.
15. He was prohibited to enter the temple.
16. You should abstain to drink now.
17. He intends to go to Jaipur.
18. It is very difficult to dissuade him to go there.
19. He is fortunate to get a ticket.
20. I am hopeful to achieve success.

Exercise 7

Fill in the blanks with the correct prepositions chosen from the pairs given in brackets :

1. We played a joke .... him. (of, on)
2. Who else has access .... the computer files? (of, to)
3. I have no recollection .... the event. (of, on)
4. Missing the bus is no excuse .... being late. (for, of)

5. I have confidence .... his ability. (for, in)
6. That is only one example ....what I mean. (in, of)
7. Pay close attention.........the traffic signals. (for, to)
8. She takes an active interest .... community events. (in, of)
9. Do you have any proof ....that? (of, to)
10. You should make allowances .... their lack of experience. (for, on)
11. There is a lack .... information on this subject. (for, of)
12. The report should shed some light .... the situation. (for, on)
13. He has a talent .... putting people at ease. (for, with)
14. I received no reply .... my letter. (on, to)
15. We soon took command .... the situation. (of, with)
16. They are constantly finding fault .... other people. (of, with)
17. I have faith .... their good intentions. (in, to)
18. She has a reputation ....having the ability to deal with any situation. (for, of)
19. People often make fun .... what they do not understand. (of, to)
20. We will take a survey......... the participants. (of, on)
21. Do you have any objection .... my plan? (on, to)
22. She has a good attitude .... her job. (of, towards)

Exercise 8

Correct the following sentences :

1. She was neither ashamed nor sorry for her misbehaviour.
2. She neither objected nor approved of it.
3. Ram has no interest and passion for cricket.
4. We must prevent damage and theft of public property.
5. Please listen and reflect on this topic afterwards.
6. He asked from her a silly question.
7. The police investigated into the case.
8. Ram resembles to his father.
9. She resigned from her post.
10. Ram signed to the agreement.
11. The poet described about the nature.
12. She must love to her children.

13. We have discussed on the merits of the issue.
14. In this article, the author has described about poverty.
15. She criticized upon my action without logic.

Exercises 9

Fill in the blanks with the suitable prepositions :

1. As the restaurant is usually crowded, it is advisable to make reservations......... advance.
2. Because we have no vehicle, we go everywhere ....foot.
3. She was .... breath after running up the long flight of stairs.
4. We walked out of the room......... tiptoe, so as not to disturb the sleeping baby.
5. Inside your identity card, you should write the name of your next......... kin.
6. We made out the report .... duplicate.
7. Citrus fruits, ... example; oranges and lemons, require a long growing season.
8. The movie seemed to go on forever, but ....last it was over.
9. She is so busy, she always seems to be .... a hurry.
10. Many people believe that birds are incapable of reasoning, but .... fact, some birds are quite intelligent.
11. Since he is not very trustworthy, I advise you to take what he says .... a pinch of salt.
12. I went to the library, but the book I wanted was out ....loan.
13. We usually buy flour and rice .... bulk.
14. Since she could offer us no proof, we had to take her story .... trust.
15. He knows hundreds of poems ....heart.
16. Since we cannot find a place to live, ...the time being, we are staying at a cheap hotel.
17. Little .... little, the clouds dispersed and the sun became brighter.
18. Because of its importance, we studied the report ....detail.
19. All of the clothes sold in that store are made .... hand.
20. At an intersection, pedestrians usually have the right .... way.
21. She wants to leave .... once.
22. I brought the wrong book.........mistake.

Exercise 10

Fill in the blanks with appropriate prepositions :

1. Morning walk is beneficial .... health.
2. You are not eligible .... this post.
3. I find no exception .... this rule of grammar.
4. She has a great passion .... natural beauty.
5. You are very weak .... mathematics.
6. Suitable reward is an important incentive....... hard work.
7. I am sick....................... the whole episode.
8. He insisted .... complaining against the officer.
9. You are to conform .... the rules of the institute.
10. Your views don't accord .... mine.
11. She comes .... a very noble family.
12. His path is beset .... many difficulties.
13. You are addicted .... gambling.
14. Your scheme is adverse .... my career.
15. The court has restored the property .... its true owner.

Exercise 11

Fill in the blanks with appropriate prepositions :

1. This is subsequent .... my application dated 5th July.
2. This is consequent .... your application dated 5th July.
3. I am fond .... reading the newspaper.
4. You have made all preparations .... the marriage.
5. I am proud .... my heritage.
6. He is a descendant .... the king.
7. I have no trust .... him.
8. She has distrust...................... you.
9. I feel ashamed .... her conduct.
10. I am much ashamed .... my son.
11. We must provide .... the bad days.
12. God will provide .... our necessities.
13. It is expected .... you to find the solution.
14. Such rude behaviour was not expected .... you.
15. I am disappointed ....you.

Exercise 12

Fill in the blanks with appropriate prepositions :

1. She jumped .... the well.
2. There was no student .... the class.
3. He ran .... the room.
4. Ram is sitting .... the kitchen.
5. He lives .... Delhi.
6. Please close your office.................... 9.30 pm positively.
7. She goes for a walk .... the morning, daily.
8. He is .... the top.
9. Please sit .... the green chair.
10. The dog jumped .... the cat.
11. She is sitting .... the roof.
12. The letter was written ....Shyam.
13. He wrote a letter .... a pen.
14. A Banyan tree stands .... the Yamuna river.
15. He has a car, ... a scooter.
16. I will go to school .... next Monday.
17. I know Hindi, ... Punjabi.
18. I haven't seen her .... the last three days.
19. I haven't seen her .... January.
20. She turned pale .... fear.

Exercise 13

Fill in the blanks appropriately with the following prepositions:

[for, to, at, in, during, with, from, between, against, over, without, after, towards, about, on]

1. Since late 1960's or early 1970's, politicians have been getting tough .....crime.
2. Every prisoner going through the system has his own thoughts ....this insane environment.
3. Most of you are not sympathetic .... me.
4. The jurors glared at them......open hostility during the entire trial.
5. He should still have the opportunity to appeal even ....such a long delay.

6. I agree with you..........that point.
7. It is easier to think and write ....any distractions.
8. You must have a metal detector passed..........your body, making sure that you are not smuggling weapons out with you.
9. It lowers the light's intensity and protects ...... ultraviolet rays.
10. There is no difference .... weekdays, the weekends and holidays.
11. Everybody wears the black suit ....the heist.
12. I am sure that it has effectively cut off many prisoners ....their friends and families.
13. A large number of people, who are anti-abortion, are most adamantly ......the death penalty.
14. My favourite breakfast is instant potatoes covered ....gravy.
15. They turned their backs..........me when I needed them most.
16. I explained to them.......... American attitude .... people in prison.
17. Many people draw comparisons between what happened ....the OJ trial and what I have been through.
18. The environment of prison was totally alien ......anything he had ever been exposed to in the past.
19. The movie, "Saptarishi" has grossed over Rs. 100 lacs ....the box office.
20. They are cheering the fact that they have survived ....another year.

Exercise 14

Fill in the blanks with the prepositions; 'for', 'during' or 'while', in the following sentences:

1. What did Ram say about me .... I was out of the room?
2. Rahim read a number of books and magazines .... he was ill.
3. I went out for dinner last night. Unfortunately, I began to feel sick .... the meal and had to go home.
4. Please don't interrupt me .... I am speaking.
5. There were many interruptions .... the Chairman's speech.
6. Can you lay the table .... I get the dinner ready?
7. They hadn't had anything to eat .... they were travelling.
8. Manisha was very angry with me. She didn't speak to me .... a week.

9. We usually go out at weekend, but we don't often go out .... the week.
10. Kamlesh started a new job a few weeks ago. Before that, he was out of work .... six months.
11. I need a change. I think I'll go away...........a few days.
12. The Chairman delivered a long speech. He spoke...........three hours.
13. We were hungry when we came. We hadn't had anything to eat...........the journey.
14. We were hungry when we came. We hadn't had anything to eat...........eight hours.
15. We met a lot of people...................we were on holiday.
16. We met a lot of people....................our holiday.
17. I met Manisha......................I was shopping.
18. ....we were in Agra, we stayed at a very comfortable hotel.
19. ....our stay in Agra, we visited a lot of museums and galleries.
20. The phone rang three times...................... they were having dinner.
21. The phone range many times .... the night.
22. I had been away for many years, ...that period, many things had changed.

Exercises 15

Fill in the blanks with the correct prepositions chosen from those given in the brackets :

1. He lives ....19, Tower Road. (at, on)
2. We will be gone .... two days. (for, since)
3. Tom and his friend will divide the money.........themselves. (among, between)
4. They will be returning .... November. (in, on)
5. I have known him ....three years. (for, since)
6. Many food items, ... milk, contain calcium. (beside, besides)
7. I will arrive .... six o'clock. (at, in)
8. He has been away .... Friday. (for, since)
9. The store is located .... North Street. (at, on)
10. She is leaving .... five minutes. (at, in)

11. Bridget, Leslie and Sarah will discuss the matter ....themselves. (among, between)

12. I have known her .... last year. (for, since)

13. We expect them .... Wednesday. (in, on)

14. The cat was sitting ....the stove. (beside, besides)

15. The play begins......... seven thirty. (at, on)

16. We waited ....fifteen minutes. (for, since)

17. Columbus crossed the Atlantic ....1492. (at, in)

18. There are many possibilities, ... the ones I have mentioned. (beside, besides)

19. She will call us.........half an hour. (at, in)

20. His birthday is .... the 8th of January. (in, on)

21. They live .... 359 Southdale Avenue. (at, on)

22. The meeting will take place .... Tuesday. (at, on)

23. We have been travelling .... several days. (for, since)

24. She has been working ....six o'clock this morning. (for, since)

Exercise 16

Fill in the blanks with the prepositions; 'by' or 'until', in the following sentences:

1. I'm moving into my new house next month. I'm staying with a friend..................then.
2. Sorry, but I must go. I have to be at home latest ....9 o'clock .
3. I've been offered a lucrative job ...... my friend. I haven't decided yet whether to accept it or not. I have to decide it ....next Monday.
4. I think I'll wait .... Sunday before making a final decision.
5. It's too late to go shopping. The shops are open only .... 9.30. They'll be closed .... now.
6. I'd better pay the electricity bill. It has to be paid .... tomorrow positively.
7. Don't pay the bill today, wait ....next Monday, you can get some relief.

8. A : Have you finished redecorating your house?

   B : Not yet. We hope to finish .... the end of this fortnight.

9. A : I'm going out now. I'll be back at 7.30. Will you still be there?

   B : I don't think so. I'll probably have gone out .... then.

10. Suresh has gone away. He'll be away ....Saturday.

Exercise 17

Fill in the blanks with the following prepositions:
[for, about, in, from, into, until, with, of, to, on]

1. The film leaves the viewer .... a warm-hearted feeling towards the inmates.
2. "The Dollars Redemption" is one of the few films this year to refrain .... insulting the viewers.
3. This film is considered the dark horse......... the Oscar Award.
4. Rahul is sentenced .... murder to two life terms.
5. Ramesh and Anita share a value system that is rooted .... restraint.
6. Chris settles......... the monotony of life without hope.
7. It is a routine ....explosions alternating ....boredom.
8. This is an extraordinary movie .... hope, friendship, and suffering in life.
9. The film is carefully constructed and shot ....an even pace.
10. Longman's Blue is the anchor that keeps us from sinking .... a sea of emotion.
11. Cindrella bets .... a tall, lanky guy named Jacky.
12. He is thrown......... solitary confinement.
13. Dinesh was sick ....the bureaucracy, the Roman Catholic Church had become.
14. He is constantly losing the battle .... his parishioners.
15. Mathew was dedicated to liberating the lower-class English congregation .... the class structure that oppressed them.
16. The story is told ....flashback.
17. The plot is unpredictable .... the credits roll.
18. There are six elements crucial.........an effective trick.
19. "The Triple Murder", can be viewed as the cinematic equivalent......... a magic trick.
20. Ram and Rahim deserve praise .... their effort.

Exercise 18

Fill in the blanks with the prepositions; 'at', 'on' or 'in', in the following sentences:

1. The telephone and the doorbell rang.................... the same time.
2. Harish and Sarla always go out for a meal .... their wedding anniversary.
3. Ramu is 58. He'll be retiring from his job .... two years' time.
4. I've been invited to a wedding .... 15th August.
5. Hurry up! We've got to go .... five minutes.
6. I'm busy just now but I'll be with you .... a moment.
7. Ram's brother is a banker but he's out of work........... the moment.
8. There are usually a lot of parties .... New Year's Eve.
9. I hope the weather will be nice.................the weakened.
10. We travelled overnight to London and arrived .... 5 o'clock.................the morning.
11. The course begins...................... 27th June and ends sometime...................... August.
12. It was quite a short novel and easy to read. I read it .... a day.
13. He might not be at home .....Tuesday morning but he'll probably be there ......the afternoon.
14. My jeep is being repaired at the garage. It will be ready .... two hours.

Exercise 19

Fill in blanks suitably with the following prepositions:

[about, for, in, up, against, by, into, of, out, to, on]

1. All the applicants had to wait .... a reply from the company.
2. They showed ....at the party without having been invited.
3. He always dreamt .... being a famous actor.
4. The judge ruled in favour .... the plaintiff.
5. He is fond .... chocolates.
6. She is longing......... her boyfriend to return from overseas.
7. They involved themselves .... the demonstration.
8. The effective use.........references will get students a higher grade.

9. Mavis was sitting .... the edge of the bed.

10. Leon took ....a knife from his pocket, and dropped it .... his bag.

11. He took no pleasure ....punishing the children, even when they didn't care......... it.

12. He was hired ....the company to host a new show.

13. The owner had been accused......... using a legal loophole to charge high rents.

14. The police are drawing ....a security blueprint in preparation for an influx of world leaders.........the World Trade Conference.

15. The Consumer Council is taking action .... dishonest modelling agencies.

16. The President will keep an eye .... how things develop.

17. Hilda prefers tea .... coffee.

18. Mark apologized to everyone ....coming late.

Exercise 20

Fill in blanks with the correct prepositions from the following:

[for, in, up, with, down, of, out, from, on]

1. He prefers to deal.........the computer matters himself.
2. She helped her husband to build......... the business.
3. He is looking.........someone he can truly love.
4. The picture hangs ....the wall over there.
5. Douglas found himself caught.........the middle of a violent storm.
6. It is hard to figure.........how to answer all these questions.
7. Mum is preparing dinner ....the whole family.
8. Danny fell passionately ....love with Annie.
9. He is the one who battles ....justice.
10. This book is about how we can take control.........our lives.
11. American and Russian soldiers sat and drank vodka with each other ....an atmosphere of warmth and friendship.
12. Batman returns to seek ....and destroy the most savage criminals in the city.
13. David tends to quarrel ....his girlfriend over small things.
14. The children who grew up ....the neighbourhood shared many happy times together.

15. The whole neighbourhood where Jack lives is heavily infested.........rats.
16. He felt that the burden had been lifted.........his shoulders.
17. The police tried to find .... who stole his car.
18. Under his uncle's influence, he became caught.........in enthusiasm for collecting coins.
19. Having been let ....in the past, she has almost given .... on men.
20. His poetry moved us.........its quiet dignity.

Exercise 21

Fill in the blanks suitably with the following prepositions:

[for, in, at, up, with, off, of, out, to, on]

1. Nobody likes waiting.........the traffic lights.
2. I'll have to ask my mother......... money.
3. He solved the problem......... the aid of his friends.
4. My friend agreed .... lend me some books.
5. His love for Mexico is based ....the friendliness of the Mexicans.
6. He apologized to his grandmother ....having to ask her for more money.
7. The products are tested ....updated utilities.
8. They wanted their teacher to comment .... their project.
9. I'm longing .... a holiday.
10. The boy was charged ....a long list of juvenile crimes.
11. Jack specialized ....drawing animals.
12. This letter is ....Tim.
13. The injured man was.........great pain.
14. She was accused ....helping the robbers.
15. The old man signed ....for the dancing lessons.
16. In order to pay ....his debts, he has to work day and night.
17. Self-esteem, as it turns ...., is a big subject in American classrooms.
18. I'm tired of waiting ....the others.
19. Jerry is afraid......... snakes.
20. Jim is never.........time.

Exercise 22

Fill in the appropriate preposition in the following sentences:

1. The poor have to work .... morning to evening.

(a) in (b) to

(c) from (d) before

2. I go .... swim every morning.

(a) to (b) for

(c) at (d) in

3. Never laugh .... the disabled.

(a) on (b) from

(c) to (d) at

4. Please wait .... me, I am coming within five minutes.

(a) for (b) by

(c) from (d) to

5. He fell .... love with Sakshi.

(a) by (b) for

(c) in (d) with

6. I got your parcel .... Tuesday.

(a) since (b) for

(c) to (d) on

7. She was married .... an early age.

(a) for (b) of

(c) at (d) in

8. His father died .... the age of sixty three.

(a) at (b) in

(c) for (d) of

9. They will go to Bangalore ....a plane.

(a) on (b) in

(c) by (d) from

10. The man .... a beard is my brother.

(a) in (b) of

(c) for (d) with

11. I am grateful .... my friends for their moral support.

(a) for (b) to

(c) of (d) with

12. Gandhiji fought .... the freedom of our country.

(a) by (b) in

(c) of (d) for

13. This watch is a gift .... my uncle.

(a) by (b) from

(c) of (d) in

14. He spoke .... the subject for two hours regularly.

(a) in (b) on

(c) of (d) with

15. They will leave the place .... 10 pm.

(a) on (b) since

(c) for (d) at

Exercise 23

Fill in the blanks appropriately with the following prepositions:

[for, as, in, from, at, over, with, of, behind, to, around, on]

1. The Indians have to adapt .... many changes.
2. That girl has grown .... six feet.
3. English immersion programme is popular with students from the province .... Quebec.
4. They want to understand the world .... them.
5. All the students in one class need to be .... approximately the same level of English proficiency.
6. The methods .... data collection included; observation, interviews and questionnaires.
7. We will now move .... to discuss the methodology and approach adopted.
8. .... the past decade, there has been a great change in China's economic policies.
9. China's economic growth lagged far .... much of the rest of the world up to 1970's.
10. The income tax is fixed .... the rate of 15%.

11. Firms are provided relatively free market environment .... minimal government intervention.

12. The average income in the Special Economic Zones now ranks .... the higest in China.

13. John taught English to classes in which students .... different cultural backgrounds were mixed together.

14. Mary produced a 50 page general introduction .... a 100 page thesis.

15. Marks were deducted .... irrelevance of ideas.

16. The Oriental pattern may be detected .... the English writing not only of Chinese students, but also of most South-East Asian people.

17. A ship is harboured .... San Pedro, California.

18. Hong Kong students prefer working in learning groups outside .... the classroom.

19. .... all the subjects .... the school curriculum, perhaps the most difficult subject is the study of language.

20. The paper has two sections, ... equal weighting.

Exercise 24

Tick the appropriate preposition in each of the following sentences:

1. She was punished .... stealing a saree.

   (a) for (b) by

   (c) with (d) from

2. The box belonged .... the landlord.

   (a) of (b) with

   (c) to (d) for

3. You must finish your project .... 5 o'clock positively.

   (a) in (b) for

   (c) till (d) to

4. Children are fond .... chocolates and computer games.

   (a) for (b) of

   (c) with (d) in

5. We get rains .... July every year.

   (a) for (b) to

   (c) on (d) in

6. His father died .... cancer.

(a) in (b) of

(c) by (d) for

7. He is not popular .... the students.

(a) by (b) among

(c) with (d) at

8. She has great love .... her children

(a) for (b) of

(c) by (d) with

9. He was prevented .... going to college.

(a) to (b) of

(c) by (d) from

10. Listen .... what your teachers say.

(a) at (b) in

(c) to (d) for

11. Please beware .... the dog.

(a) of (b) with

(c) to (d) for

12. This book is a collection .... Shakespeare's poems.

(a) for (b) of

(c) with (d) by

13. They have quarrelled .... a piece of land.

(a) at (b) on

(c) for (d) over

Exercise 25

Fill in the blanks appropriately with the following prepositions:

[away, behind, from, for, on, over, into, up, of, to, about, in]

1. She called to me ....assistance.
2. He jumped ....his car and drove away.
3. With no one to help her, she has to do everything .... her own.
4. The house is built .... wood and bricks.
5. He is blind .... one eye.

6. As the day, hours and minutes swiftly tick .... , Bruce uses every legal strategy to win clemency .... his grandfather.
7. She kept banging .... the door until someone answered.
8. There's a cockroach .... the ceiling.
9. He met a mysterious figure who knew the truth .... the crime.
10. She is willing to help others and shows concern .... them.
11. He has just broken .... with his girlfriend and is .... his own.
12. Many people feel uneasy ....the situation in Afghanistan.
13. The small child found himself trapped ....a big hole.
14. Lily revived .... a coma.
15. She was put .... jail.
16. The customer complained to the manager .... the terrible service.
17. The film offers a rare glimpse .... an uncommon romance.
18. He was so desperate that he resorted .... violence.
19. The workers have cast doubt .... whether they have received fair treatment.
20. The woman attributed the death of her son .... poor medical treatment.

Exercise 26

Fill in the blanks appropriately with the following prepositions:

[about, down, for, in, at, up, with, against, by, into, off, of, out, to, on]

1. Try not to lean.........the computer desk.
2. Nobody is willing to talk ....politics.
3. They are aware.........the pollution problems.
4. June is always able to put words ....action.
5. The manufacturers are trying to speed ....the process of production.
6. She met him ....Kai Tak airport.
7. The driver should not be blamed.........the death of his co-passenger.
8. Lilian had to cut ....her workload in order to have more free time.
9. The residents urged the owner of the building to set a deadline .... clearance.
10. The students were told to polish.........their computer skills.
11. They tried to work ....the answer.

12. The couple called.........the engagement last week.
13. The old woman is......... her way to catch a flight to Canada.
14. Stella applied .... a job after her graduation.
15. Readers can search .... different types of books by computer.
16. All the students were greatly inspired ....their teacher.
17. He always keeps in touch ....his grandmother.
18. Many popular movies are based ....best-selling books.
19. He attempted to get revenge .... his enemy.
20. It makes me feel uncomfortable when people stare .... me.

Exercise 27

Fill in the blanks appropriately with the following prepositions:

[for, at, over, to, from, until, on, in, with, by, than, into, of]

1. Normal concrete consists .... cement, aggregate and water.
2. He occasionally indulges .... the luxury of a good cigar.
3. Cars pump millions of tonnes of carbon dioxide......... the atmosphere every year.
4. His interest .... building up a network of companies is strong.
5. This new technique is superior ....the old one.
6. The candidate must have at least three years of professional experience .... organizing.
7. Sega has turned .... Microsoft to develop an operating system.
8. We know .... experience that we can increase sales .... advertising.
9. So far he has spent 750 million dollars .... this project.
10. Cellular phones are sold .... half the price.
11. The tallest buildings in London are small in comparison .... those in New York.
12. Nintendo's game is not due......... the autumn of 2008.
13. Although the programmer had taken the rotation of the Earth ....account, he had forgotten that the Earth also rotates round the sun.
14. On the Faroe islands, they insist .... continuing with their barbaric slaughter of whales.
15. These people live, ... a great extent, by fishing.

16. One should not even mention the competitors .... name.

17. The semi-conductor business is different ....the business of building big computers.

18. "Face Off" is a massive improvement .... Woo's first two North Amercian films.

19. Cops and gangsters were forced to confront their affinities ....each other.

20. Troy goes .... a coma before telling Archer where he planted the nerve-gas bomb.

Exercise 28

Fill in the blanks appropriately with the following prepositions:

[for, in, up, with, down, to, out, by, on]

1. Brian's father was preoccupied.........his stamp collection.
2. Peggy has tried several times to give .... smoking, but she can't.
3. They hope to increase contacts .... other universities in China.
4. The illegal factories were shut ....
5. The pirates were all sentenced.........death.
6. The girl is.........trial for murdering a young boy.
7. Teenagers rarely turn .... their parents or teachers for advice.
8. The doctor had to explain.........full what the cancer treatment involved.
9. The information will be passed ....to the police.
10. Eric participates ....the school' s athletics team.
11. On his birthday, he drank wine ....the first time.
12. The questionnaire asked students about everything, from habits of personal hygiene,.........how they cope with a crisis.
13. The research assistants handed ....the questionnaire to the students.
14. Children should ask ....their parents' help when they meet difficulties.
15. The magazine is scheduled to come .... next month.
16. The electrical system broke......... just before the new block was opened.

17. The toy car was destroyed ....a naughty boy.
18. She wants to set a good example ....her son.
19. The newspaper is very interested.........that photograph.
20. Of course, he cares ....his children's safety.

Exercise 29

Tick the correct preposition in the following sentences:

1. She wants to get rid ....the brown fox.
   (a) for (b) to
   (c) with (d) of
2. I was invited .... tea by his mother.
   (a) for (b) to
   (c) with (d) in
3. You cannot see germs .... naked eyes.
   (a) by (b) with
   (c) for (d) in
4. He is not interested .... playing and skiing.
   (a) in (b) for
   (c) by (d) of
5. He was fast asleep .... his bed
   (a) into (b) in
   (c) by (d) for
6. We have a very good news .... him.
   (a) for (b) of
   (c) to (d) with
7. They have been reading .... 7 o'clock
   (a) for (b) in
   (c) since (d) at
8. Never quarrel .... your friends.
   (a) to (b) with
   (c) by (d) over
9. The four brothers always quarrelled .... themselves.
   (a) to (b) between
   (c) for (d) among

10. There were several policemen .... duty on the Republic Day.

(a) to (b) on

(c) for (d) at

11. These boys go to college .... the college bus.

(a) by (b) on

(c) to (d) for

12. He is not an honest man. You cannot rely .... him.

(a) to (b) for

(c) at (d) on

13. He was fined .... driving negligently.

(a) to (b) of

(c) by (d) for

14. He is often late .... his dinner.

(a) for (b) at

(c) to (d) in

15. Try to reach the village .... the sunset.

(a) before (b) by

(c) from (d) of

Exercise 30

Fill in the blanks appropriately with the following prepositions:

[for, to, by, in, during, with, around, of, off, about, on]

1. She blackmails the men to perform some dirty work........a pier in New York.
2. Students should change in order to succeed........a western- style college.
3. From beginning to the end, the story is overwhelmed .... style.
4. They were brought in for a policc line-up and questioned .... a heist.
5. This crime involves 17 men and 19 million dollars .... cocaine.
6. The movie revolves ....seven criminals brought together for a police line-up.

7. Britain is mostly made up of people ....different accents.
8. Lenin had a very specific vision ....each scene.
9. ....the Christmas season, the mail slows from it's usual 3-4 weeks, to 5-6 weeks.
10. Blonde tortures the cop and cuts ....his ear.
11. Blonde has the complete trust ....two Mafia bosses, and is completely loyal.........them.
12. .... a thematic level, "Reservoir Dogs" is infact a deeply moral film.
13. They have no conception........empathy ....the individuals concerned.
14. It is the torture victims themselves who actually plant the ideas ....their torturers' minds.
15. There is nothing you can do, except pray ....a quick death.
16. On Friday night, the streets are choked .... fans and paparazzi.
17. His scripts have become magnets ....many of our better younger actors.
18. He tested in the 170s ....school GK tests.
19. It was an homage ....the magazines of the 50s.
20. They are collaborating.........a Japanese film called "Twenty Hours".

Exercise 31

Tick the correct preposition in the following sentences:

1. In the month of December, the temperature falls .... 40°C.

   (a) from (b) below
   (c) at (d) into

2. A jeep hit him while he was going .... the main road.

   (a) on (b) across
   (c) behind (d) through

3. She is .... a noble family of the Rajputs.

   (a) from (b) of
   (c) among (d) at

4. The case was put .... the judge and the judge decided it within an year.

(a) at (b) from

(c) before (d) of

5. The bridge .... this river was built in the year 1995.

(a) at (b) over

(c) above (d) on

6. She is suffering .... fever.

(a) with (b) of

(c) through (d) from

7. We saw a wounded tiger while passing .... the forest.

(a) from (b) through

(c) along (d) among

8. Chairs are made .... wood.

(a) of (b) from

(c) on (d) through

9. There are tall beautiful coconut trees .... the river.

(a) along (b) at

(c) into (d) over

10. We are proud .... our children.

(a) on (b) at

(c) after (d) of

11. Mt. Abu is about five thousand feet .... the sea-level.

(a) above (b) along

(c) after (d) behind

12. His birthday is .... next Sunday.

(a) in (b) at

(c) on (d) for

13. Ramesh fell down while he was running .... a bus.

(a) into (b) after

(c) over (d) through

14. Ramesh is the best .... all the other players.

(a) into (b) among

(c) above (d) between

Exercise 32

Fill in the blanks with the appropriate ones from the following prepositions:

[for, to, towards, in, with, at, of, on]

1. He glances ....the rearview mirror of the car.
2. "Maa" is a throwback .... John's first feature.
3. With wit and imagination, the filmmakers show a rare respect ....the intelligence of their audience.
4. The people and their cars move around ....bleak, snowy landscapes.
5. In this film, Karan is playing role of a musician dying ....AIDS.
6. Pramod has a storyteller's genius .... incident and personality.
7. "A cronic Fate" would make a fine companion piece .... "Babe".
8. The intention of this book is to serve as a base ....all information concerning Clinton and Gorbachev.
9. This leads Watson .... considerations about the construction of the hall.
10. ....the stroke of midnight on New Year Eve, people will start cheering and whistling.
11. This brilliant psychiatrist plays manipulative mind games ....his victims.
12. This outgoing and enthusiastic young man excelled both academically and ....sporting achievements.
13. After reading the letter, he angrily ripped it.........shreds.
14. Alfredo taught Toto to set his sights beyond the Cinema Paradiso ....the world outside.
15. Toto's naive passion ....movies closely resembles the director's own.
16. In "Cinema Paradiso", we catch glimpses .... Charlie Chaplin and John Wayne.
17. The images can float ....a wall, there in the night above the heads of the people.
18. We are on a city street.........broad daylight.
19. John Woo has a unique eye .... some great effects and action sequences.
20. The climactic speedboat scene of "Facc Off" puts the lumbering "Speed 2".........shame.

Exercise 33

Fill in the blanks with appropriate prepositions:

1. The meeting took place .... the company's corporate office. (at/to/on/by)
2. It was a very long voyage. We were .... sea for 50 days. (in/at/on/by/to)
3. I was .... Peter's, last night. (in/on/at/by/for)
4. The train called .... Kolkata main station. (in/on/to/at/by)
5. I lost my passport .... the way to India. (in/at/by/to/on)
6. He is a genius. He is .... the black lists of many casinos. (on/in/with/by/at)
7. We reached late at the cinema so we had to sit ....the back row. (on/in/at/to/by)
8. Is there anything interesting .... the paper today? (on/by/in/at/from/)
9. Have you ever been ....Mexico? (in/on/by/to)
10. These books are .... Rs 150 each. (in/on/with/for)
11. Some people are .... prison for crimes they have not committed. (in/on/at/by/to)
12. I am really sorry but you are standing .... my way. (on/in/at/with/behind)
13. There was a very serious accident .... the roundabout. (in/at/to/from)
14. In many countries, people drive .... the left. (in/at/by/on/to)
15. I forgot my umbrella ....the bus. (in/into/by/onto/on)
16. I am .... love with her. (in/on/with/from)
17. We are offering solutions .... a price almost anyone can afford. (in/at/on/by/through)
18. He behaves just like his father. He really takes .... him. (to/from/after/by/at)
19. That old house is being offered .... sale. (in/at/on/for/by)
20. It is very difficult to enter .... partnership with a person you do not know very well. (to/on/by/with/into)

Exercises 34

Fill in the blanks with the correct prepositions chosen from the pairs given in the brackets:

1. We are ready ....anything. (for, to)
2. I was anxious ....her. (about, to)
3. Photographic film is sensitive......... light. (of, to)
4. Seals are adapted ....life in the water. (at, to)
5. He is descended .... Mary, Queen of Scots. (from, of)
6. Cotton is more resistant .... fire than nylon is. (for, to)
7. After the show, the radio station was besieged .... telephone calls. (from, with)
8. She was praised......... her achievements. (for, to)
9. The public library is accessible ....everyone. (to, with)
10. Are you familiar......... the procedures? (for, with)
11. They were overjoyed .... the news. (at, to)
12. We are proud ....our accomplishments. (for, of)
13. I was pleased ....the results. (of, with)
14. Are you aware .... the risks involved? (of, with)
15. Lack of exercise can be detrimental .... one's health. (of, to)
16. We are satisfied ....the arrangement. (for, with)
17. She is interested ....animals. (for, in)
18. He is well qualified ....the job. (for, to)
19. Young children are often suspicious ....strangers. (of, to)
20. Knowledge of mathematics is essential .... an engineer. (to, with)
21. We were curious......... what they were doing. (about, for)
22. The design of most computers is based .... binary arithmetic. (for, on)

Exercise 35

Fill in the blanks appropriately with the following prepositions:

[for, in, at, into, by, of, off, to, about, on]

1. America has ceded key technologies.........Pakistan.
2. Even a speck.........dust can cause fatal damage.
3. TV has a bad influence .... the youth.

4. They have already lost the battle .... microchips.
5. These tiny machines may some day be configured ....motors that will guide tiny rockets.
6. The set consists ....pens and various drawing tools.
7. It is a proof ....the experiment's validity.
8. There may be some inconsistency ....the rules.
9. Glucose is oxidised......... the tips of tiny electrodes.
10. It is measured ....billionths of a metre.
11. Each of the chips was about one inch.........size.
12. They have a one ....fifty chance of success.
13. The supplier must respond......... customer demand.
14. There is much more.........corporate ideology than efficient manufacturing.
15. They can increase sales.........advertising.
16. Technology is giving way ....organisation in terms of improving manufacturing.
17. Companies move abroad in search ....cheap labour.
18. Sony is more concerned ....reducing transit time.
19. The quality standards prevailing .... American industry are not good enough.
20. One measure of quality is the number of sets that come .... the end of the production line without defects.

ANSWERS

Exercise 1

1. to **2.** of **3.** via **4.** from **5.** off **6.** like **7.** out of **8.** with **9.** until **10.** past **11.** of **12.** but **13.** opposite **14.** Despite **15.** under **16.** before **17.** without **18.** into **19.** during **20.** along **21.**about **22.** between.

Exercise 2

1. for **2.** on **3.** to **4.** at **5.** on **6.** from **7.** for **8.** in **9.** towards **10.** in/with **11.** on **12.** against **13.** after **14.** along **15.** to **16.** into **17.** to **18.** on **19.** in, with **20.** into.

Exercise 3

1. from **2.** on **3.** from **4.** on **5.** against **6.** of **7.** for **8.** in **9.** for **10.** of **11.** to **12.** at **13.** from **14.** with **15.** from **16.** for **17.** in **18.** at **19.** for **20.** on **21.** to **22.** with

Exercise 4

1. with **2.** at **3.** at **4.** over **5.** by **6.** up **7.** on **8.** of **9.** in **10.** on **11.** up **12.** on **13.** with **14.** out **15.** out.

Exercise 5

1. in **2.** for **3.** of **4.** beside **5.** to **6.** after **7.** of **8.** upon/off **9.** along **10.** into **11.** to **12.** for **13.** by **14.** at **15.** into, beside.

Exercise 6

1. You cannot prevent me from going to the market.
2. She refrains from doing this work.

3. I insisted him on attending the class.
4. He has a passion for learning English grammar.
5. She is negligent in attending the meetings.
6. She persisted in writing again.
7. He is bent on fighting again.
8. I am confident of winning the match.
9. He succeeded in passing the examination this time.
10. I am proud of having a friend like Ram.
11. I cannot hinder her from entering the temple.
12. She is desirous of leaving the place.
13. Raju was disqualified from competing in this tournament.
14. I cannot think of opposing him.
15. He was prohibited from entering the temple.
16. You should abstain from drinking now.
17. He intends on going to Jaipur.
18. It is very difficult to dissuade him from going there.
19. He is fortunate in getting a ticket.
20. I am hopeful of achieving success.

Exercise 7

1. on **2.** to **3.** of **4.** for **5.** in **6.** of **7.** to **8.** in
9. of **10.** for **11.** of **12.** on **13.** for **14.** to **15.** of
16. with **17.** in **18.** for **19.** of **20.** of **21.** to
22. towards.

Exercise 8

1. She was neither ashamed of nor sorry for her misbehaviour.
2. She neither objected to nor approved of it.
3. Ram has no interest in and passion for cricket.
4. We must prevent damage to and theft of public property.
5. Please listen to and reflect on this topic afterwards.

6. He asked her a silly question.
7. The police investigated the case.
8. Ram resembles his father.
9. She resigned her post.
10. Ram signed the agreement.
11. The poet described the nature.
12. She must love her children.
13. We have discussed the merits of the issue.
14. In this article, the author has described poverty.
15. She criticised my action without logic.

Exercise 9

1. in **2.** on **3.** out of **4.** on **5.** of **6.** in **7.** for **8.** at **9.** in **10.** in **11.** with **12.** on **13.** in **14.** on **15.** by **16.** for **17.** by **18.** in **19.** by **20.** of **21.** at **22.** by.

Exercise 10

1. to **2.** for **3.** to **4.** for **5.** in **6.** to **7.** of **8.** on **9.** to **10.** with **11.** from **12.** with **13.** to **14.** to **15.** to.

Exercise 11

1. to **2.** upon **3.** of **4.** for **5.** of **6.** of **7.** in **8.** of **9.** at **10.** of **11.** against **12.** for **13.** of **14.** from **15.** in.

Exercise 12

1. into **2.** in **3.** into **4.** in **5.** in **6.** at **7.** in **8.** at **9.** on **10.** upon **11.** on **12.** by **13.** with **14.** beside **15.** besides **16.** from **17.** besides **18.** for **19.** since **20.** with.

Exercise 13

1. on **2.** about **3.** towards **4.** in **5.** after **6.** on **7.** without **8.** over **9.** against **10.** between **11.** during **12.** from **13.** for **14.** with/in **15.** on **16.** about, towards **17.** in **18.** to **19.** at **20.** for.

Exercise 14

1. while **2.** while **3.** during **4.** while **5.** during **6.** while **7.** while **8.** for **9.** during **10.** for **11.** for **12.** for **13.** during **14.** for **15.** while **16.** during **17.** while **18.** while **19.** during **20.** while **21.** during **22.** during.

Exercise 15

1. at **2.** for **3.** between **4.** in **5.** for **6.** besides **7.** at **8.** since **9.** on **10.** in **11.** among **12.** since **13.** on **14.** beside **15.** at **16.** for **17.** in **18.** besides **19.** in **20.** on **21.** at **22.** on **23.** for **24.** since.

Exercise 16

1. until **2.** by **3.** by, by, **4.** until **5.** until, by **6.** by **7.** until **8.** by **9.** by **10.** until.

Exercise 17

1. with **2.** from **3.** for **4.** for **5.** in **6.** into **7.** of, with **8.** about **9.** with **10.** in **11.** on **12.** into **13.** of **14.** with **15.** from **16.** in **17.** until **18.** to **19.** of **20.** for.

Exercise 18

1. at **2.** on **3.** in **4.** on **5.** in **6.** in **7.** at **8.** on **9.** at **10.** at, in **11.** on, in **12.** in **13.** on, in **14.** in.

Exercise 19

1. for **2.** up **3.** of **4.** of **5.** of **6.** for **7.** in **8.** of
9. on **10.** out, into **11.** in, about **12.** by **13.** of
14. up, for **15.** against **16.** on **17.** to **18.** for.

Exercise 20

1. with **2.** up **3.** for **4.** on **5.** in **6.** out **7.** for
8. in **9.** for **10.** of **11.** in **12.** out **13.** with **14.** in
15. with **16.** from/off **17.** out **18.** up **19.** down, up
20. with.

Exercise 21

1. at **2.** for **3.** with **4.** to **5.** on **6.** for **7.** with
8. on **9.** for **10.** with **11.** in **12.** for **13.** in **14.** of
15. up **16.** off **17.** out **18.** for **19.** of **20.** on.

Exercise 22

1. (c) **2.** (b) **3.** (d) **4.** (a) **5.** (c) **6.** (d) **7.** (c)
8. (a) **9.** (c) **10.** (d) **11.** (b) **12.** (d) **13.** (b)
14. (b) **15.** (d)

Exercise 23

1. to **2.** to **3.** of **4.** around **5.** at **6.** for **7.** on
8. over **9.** behind **10.** at **11.** with **12.** as **13.** from
14. to **15.** for **16.** in **17.** in **18.** of **19.** of, on **20.** of.

Exercise 24

1. (a) **2.** (c) **3.** (c) 4. (b) **5.** (d) **6.** (b) **7.** (c)
8. (a) **9.** (d) **10.** (c) **11.** (a) **12.** (b) **13.** (d)

Exercise 25

1. for **2.** into/in **3.** on **4.** of **5.** in **6.** away/by, for

7. on **8.** on **9.** behind/about **10.** for **11.** up, on

12. about **13.** in/inside **14.** from **15.** in/into **16.** about
17. of **18.** to **19.** on **20.** to.

Exercise 26

1. against **2.** about **3.** of **4.** into **5.** up **6.** at **7.** for
8. down **9.** for **10.** up **11.** out **12.** off **13.** on **14.** for
15. for **16.** by **17.** with **18.** on **19.** on **20.** at.

Exercise 27

1. of **2.** in **3.** into **4.** in **5.** to **6.** in **7.** to
8. from, by **9.** on **10.** at/for **11.** with **12.** until
13. into **14.** on **15.** to **16.** by **17.** from/than
18. over/on **19.** for/with **20.** into

Exercise 28

1. with 2. up **3.** with **4.** down **5.** to **6.** on **7.** to
8. in **9.** on **10.** in **11.** for **12.** to **13.** out **14.** for
15. out **16.** down **17.** by **18.** for/to **19.** in
20. for/about.

Exercise 29

1. (d) **2.** (b) **3.** (b) **4.** (a) **5.** (b) **6.** (a) **7.** (c)
8. (b) **9.** (d) **10.** (b) **11.** (a) **12.** (d) **13.** (d)
14. (a) **15.** (a)

Exercise 30

1. on **2.** in **3.** by **4.** about **5.** in **6.** around 7. with
8. for **9.** during **10.** off **11.** of, to **12.** on **13.** of, with
14. in **15.** for **16.** with **17.** for **18.** on **19.** to **20.** on

Exercise 31

1. (b) **2.** (b) **3.** (a) **4.** (c) **5.** (b) **6.** (d) **7.** (b)
8. (a) **9.** (a) **10.** (d) **11.** (a) **12.** (c) **13.** (b) **14.** (b)

Exercise 32

1. in **2.** to **3.** for **4.** in **5.** of **6.** for **7.** to **8.** for **9.** to **10.** at **11.** with **12.** in **13.** to/into **14.** towards/to **15.** for **16.** of **17.** on **18.** in **19.** for **20.** to.

Exercise 33

1. at **2.** at **3.** at **4.** at **5.** on **6.** on **7.** in **8.** in **9.** to **10.** for **11.** in **12.** in **13.** at **14.** on **15.** on **16.** in **17.** at **18.** after **19.** for **20.** into.

Exercise 34

1. for **2.** about **3.** to **4.** to **5.** from **6.** to **7.** with **8.** for **9.** to **10.** with **11.** at **12.** of **13.** with **14.** of **15.** to **16.** with **17.** in **18.** for **19.** of **20.** to **21.** about **22.** on.

Exercise 35

1. to **2.** of **3.** on **4.** for **5.** into **6.** of **7.** of **8.** in **9.** at **10.** to **11.** in **12.** in **13.** to **14.** to **15.** by **16.** to **17.** of **18.** about **19.** in **20.** off.

❍

www.ingramcontent.com/pod-product-compliance
Ingram Content Group UK Ltd.
Pitfield, Milton Keynes, MK11 3LW, UK
UKHW021657190726
13853UKWH00001B/314